AND ONE TO GROW ON

BOOKS BY JOHN GOULD

NEW ENGLAND TOWN MEETING

PRE-NATAL CARE FOR FATHERS

FARMER TAKES A WIFE

THE HOUSE THAT JACOB BUILT

AND ONE TO GROW ON

AND ONE
TO GROW ON

RECOLLECTIONS OF
A MAINE BOYHOOD
BY JOHN GOULD

Down East Books
Camden, Maine

Down East Books

An imprint of The Rowman & Littlefield Publishing Group, Inc.
4501 Forbes Blvd., Ste. 200
Lanham, MD 20706
www.rowman.com

Distributed by NATIONAL BOOK NETWORK

British Library Cataloguing in Publication Information available

Library of Congress Cataloging-in-Publication Data available

ISBN 978-1-60893-540-6 (paperback)
ISBN 978-1-60893-541-3 (e-book)

FOR R. E. BULLARD

AS TO MY TOWN . . .

SOME folks will assume my town is Freeport, Maine, but that is an unwarranted assumption. It could be any Maine tidewater town, pop. c. 2,000, back a few years, but not too many years. Personalities and places have been disguised, but sometimes not too well, and recollection is often elusive—which means that some folks may not remember what I do. The people here are real, very real; and I make no references to fictitious persons—living or dead.

J. G.

Lisbon Falls, Maine
1949

AND ONE TO GROW ON

It WASN'T geography that made my town. The geography may have made the people, but the people gave us the peculiar and distinct advantages that made my town one of the best in the State of Maine for growing-up purposes. If I tell you we had a mailman who was a spiritualist, you may not need too much additional proof. He used to stop with a letter and go into a trance and tell you what was in it. Then you'd open it up, and find that he was right. We used to read jokes about mailmen in other places who read the postcards, but that was nothing. Merle Blake knew everything, and quietly admitted it. He did, too. So we had a large assortment of folks in our town, and although all towns have their characters, no town ever had as many as we did, or such fine ones. With the perspective of later years, I know now that everybody in our town was a character—and that the town was what made character, and I know the town made mine. Whatever it may be, the town made it. All I am or ever hope to be I owe to my mother's bringing me up in that small Maine town, because growing to a man there gave me the priceless things that universities don't sell, and other people don't know.

This town taught me to walk the dusty roads barefoot and find the flowers and berries and quick-water trout. It taught me when to say what to whom, and when to keep quiet. It taught me, I suppose, all I know or ever will know—and it taught me the joy and peace and satisfaction that come to a man who knows the people around him and knows them well. Knows their whimsey and their weaknesses, their strong points and their purposes. And knows it all as a gradual absorption that came along with growing up, and was the background of everything that came later. In a small Maine town the boy has a chance.

Recollection doesn't add a thing to my town. I saw it back in the days of dirt roads, and I can see it now with the black highways running through it to the resorts. The beauty was there then, and is there now. The living has changed, but mostly because I have changed. Children still grow up there, and jump into Tooker's Brook when the days are hot, and skate on Scott's Pond when they are not, and I imagine they have the same things to learn that I did. And just as nice people to learn them from. I have seen boyhood sunrises when the ocean dripped back off the sun and all the world was bloodred with a coming storm, and I have seen them since a hundred times and they never change.

There is the town today as it was then, mostly one and the same. The little harbor, where a navy not only could lay in but in 1812 had done so, has a couple of fingering points that reach out toward the dawn, and then a broken reef of small islands that seem to dot the points and make exclamation about the loveliness of the ocean.

The old seafaring days had gone in my time, but once that harbor had sent fleets to every port. The town had moved inland a little since the days of sail, and a railroad had been built. Mills were built and the people learned trades and how to run machines. The highlanders, as Maine coastal people still call those who plow and keep store and run machines, all had so much of the ocean in them that the term was absurd. Sons whose fathers had skippered in the China Trade were growing potatoes and corn, but they could rig a vessel too, and many of them kept up their papers as master mariners of wind and steam in all waters as a token of what had sired them. The last of the sea captains were living out their lives in retired and story-telling ease, and I knew them all. We had men in our town who had been born in the rolling cabins of real Yankee ships. I went to school with Sol Gorman, whose middle name was Islands, and you can guess where a high-pooped old three-master had laid to while Mrs. Gorman had her seventh baby. Attics in my town had trunks in them filled with curiosities from all over the world, and a costume party at school was a most wonderful congregation of the races never beheld elsewhere under one roof. We had that kind of people, coming down from the previous generation, and we also had the stay-at-homes—the highlanders who didn't happen to go to sea. They might have, you know, but they didn't. My own family never had a mariner, but had been farmers and prospectors and pioneers and builders of railroads and all such land-bound things. I had no paisley shawls from far places, or tinkling bells from Oriental pagodas, or sets of sheer "chiny" that had been wedding presents from over the ocean. I did have a Sioux warclub, and a real Queen's Arm from the battle of Quebec, and the skull of an Indian who once lived in the Bad Lands, and a real gold nugget from the Klondike, and many a story of the westward course of empire—so I made out in juvenile competition, and at times my highlander trinkets outshone the more common novelties from seafaring.

Our town also had people in it who had never been anywhere. But they knew about the far places, and it was always understood that they remained at home from choice, and not because opportunity was lacking. In my town a man did as he'd a mind to, and it was all right with everybody. He *might* have gone. The woods of the state and the fields of grain and potatoes gave them a special kind of solidity, and nobody ever hung his head when exploits came up for consideration. Our farmers were just as cosmopolitan as their brothers and uncles and sons who had been to Bangkok and Calcutta, and their contributions to life in the town were just as valid. And for boys growing up, just as entertaining and instructive. Making maple syrup or Golden Russet cider was an art, too, and not one you perfected in the rigging of a brig three days down from Valparaiso.

The beauty of it was that in my time all these varied things had come together in the people, and the town had settled into a new kind of pattern that historians of New England have dismissed casually as the seedy period. Probably they are right—but we folks think going to seed can be a sedate accomplishment that all other activities of nature lead up to. Anybody knows that September is the prettiest month of the year, unless it's October, and then the warm afternoon suns help you bask and reflect, and as fullness comes to the labors of the season you can look and see that it is good. I suppose all knowledge had come to a focus in my town in my time, and if anything was worth knowing, somebody there knew it. We may have gone to seed, but things were far from in bad shape. We had good things to eat and amusing things to do, and extra-fine people to be with. There never was a time when towns in

Maine were less concerned about other towns and other places and what other people said and did. It was as if the traveler had come home, and the tired workman had put his feet up on the shelf of the kitchen stove, and knowing all things from all places, well-to-do and satisfied, had drawn his rocker a hitch closer to sit a spell. There were grandsons and nephews to gather around and listen, and much advice to be given out about the whole broad world and the futility of it. It was story time, sort of, and the stories we heard from Cap'n Ezekiel and Cap'n Ben were as nothing to the full-time stories we worked out ourselves as we grew up in such a town. We lived stories, too, and took part as this settled-down community fulfilled its happy destiny of being a small Maine town with a busy past, a contented present—and possibly a future.

We had the big old homes with widows' walks—homes built by shipwrights as they waited for the laying of another keel. There were snuggling farm stands. And the new mills had put up factory houses, all alike and painted from the same can, for the workers to buy out of payrolls. I guess we had about everything, and Maine was like that then. No matter what you wanted to do or know, there was somebody in town to turn to. We had a man who had driven a mule team in Death Valley, and a woman who swallowed swords in a circus. Her little boy used to bring the swords to school to show on Friday afternoons, and once this man had demonstrated his art when the Twenty-Mule Team Borax display came through to advertise. Everybody saw him make the long turn off Main street onto School street, and he was good. We could all see that driving a thing like that wasn't easy. We had professional story tellers in town, too, and one of them was a specialist on tales of the African jungles. He'd been there, too—but we didn't think anything of that. I don't believe there was much of anything anywhere that our town couldn't duplicate—or come close to. And usually surpass. All of this, naturally, was available to a growing boy on an intimate basis—there wasn't a soul in this whole magnificent set-up that I didn't know and couldn't speak to whenever I wanted. Not just that much, either, because I knew these people to the depths of their most intimate natures. It was the small town way. Cap'n Jim Babcock's wife wore longlegged men's underwear, and everybody knew it. "If they're too big, Annie can wear 'em," he said whenever he bought new underwear at the store, and sometimes they were too big. Besides, they hung on the washline once a week, and we could see that they were too big for the skipper. More than that, she and the skipper admitted it. Sam Treanor never smoked White Owl cigars, and we all knew that.

We knew Cap'n Jim Babcock didn't speak to his wife, either. She made him mad once, long ago, and he just stopped. She knew why, and there wasn't much she could do about it. Cap'n Jim would sit in his chair most lonesome, but stubborn, and it got to be a habit for everybody to send salesmen up to see Cap'n Jim. He had so much sales resistance he didn't even buy things he wanted, but it gave him somebody to talk to and whiled away many a lonesome afternoon. Usually the salesman was selling something a woman would like to have in the house, and while Cap'n Jim was having a demonstration, his wife would flit around looking as if she wanted one. But he never bought anything, and the whole thing worked out well because it spared the rest of the town the job of getting rid of a salesman. Ours was a time when people still did their shopping in stores, and did it in the stores in town, too. Those things register with you, can't help it, and so I grew up.

This Cap'n Jim was also the best school teacher I ever had. I told him once I was having trouble with arithmetic, and he said that was a notion. I used to take my book in after school and he'd help me with the examples. The book would say, "If A can dig a ditch in twelve hours, and B can do it in seven, how long will it take to dig a ditch if A does half and B does half," or something like that. Cap'n Jim would light his pipe and say, "You never heard of the Patricia Mae, she was lost before your time. Built here, she was, a light ship, but handy, and fast. I set a couple of records with her—one of them the Boston to Portland run. I didn't have a sail up, but we got caught in a September hurricane just out of the Boston harbor tide, and we went by Two Lights the next morning fast enough so I thought we were going right on up to Cupsuptic to shoot a deer. But the wind died, and we stood there thinking it hadn't taken very long to spend a night, and we set a record that warn't beat in my time. Well, I was in Galveston once with the Patsy-Mae, and we had a mate name of Gilligan who didn't have any more Irish in him than a Poland brood sow. He was probably named Faldetti or Ferazzo or something, but he took on Gilligan to keep out of trouble. He'd seen trouble, though, plenty of it, because he only had one eye, and that half buttoned up, and his arm on one side was crooked as a scythe snath. So this fellow come aboard one night with a big box, and he got a can of paint and wrote 'dynamite' on it and put it behind the galley stove and told nobody not to touch it. So we started off, Liverpool being our destination, and . . ."

These stories of Cap'n Jim would take the time between school-out and supper, and the upshot of each story was that the school book problem got translated into story-telling terms without changing the basic problem of the example. What we need in our schools today is a teacher who can change "Mr. A" into a one-eyed Italian cripple named Gilligan who kept a box of dynamite under a cook-stove. Then Cap'n Jim would snap a question at me that involved the price of Galveston cotton in Liverpool, and I'd give him that answer. Then it would develop that my answer was also the answer to the problem in the book, and I would go home to supper. I could change dollars into pounds, shillings and pence long before my class got into decimals—but not for my teacher. Only for Cap'n Jim. And myself. The teacher always thought I was slow at arithmetic and used to write notes home about it. My mother sometimes urged me to greater exertion, but Cap'n Jim said to never mind, that teachers didn't know everything—if they did they'd be making twice as much money at something a lot more pleasant to do.

So it wasn't the geography that made my town. Maine has reverted largely to geography since the tourist era, and fine scenery has a new value. We had fine scenery in my town, and they still have it, but we had the people, too. It's people who count. You'll find that the brooks of Maine still have some nice trout in them—but Bill Damon isn't around any more to teach you to fish them. In my time Bill Damon was not only around, but was always available. Bill was a fellow who was always either going fishing, or getting ready, and he liked company. Our town was full of people like him who had ample time to spend with anybody who happened along. So it isn't the geography I'm thinking about.

THIS is all an I Remember story, and my mother says I have too good a memory. I remember, for instance, when one of the points that ran out into our little harbor was just the back pasture of Frank Blaisdell's farm. Pastures, in Maine, have never been noted for fertility and productivity. The modern dairy specialists who advocate cultivation of pastures don't mean Maine pastures. A Maine pasture is rocks, juniper bushes, and berries. It is wild roses and sweet fern. It sometimes has grass in it, although that is not an essential quality. Maine cows are noted for their gastronomic versatility, and their owners have always felt that when they get hungry enough they'll eat anything, a feeling that many generations of farming have proved to be almost true.

So Frank Blaisdell's pasture was just an ordinary pasture in all respects except the blackcap raspberries. It was covered with blackcaps too, and there isn't anything any

nicer for jam. Ours was a blackcap town, and every summer we'd go down by the dozens and pick the blackcaps
where they'd ripened in the hot tidal sun. We had blueberries and island cranberries, and everything else, but
these blackcaps had something special about them, and
became a town tradition. There was the sweetness of seaside dews in them, and something of the salt from the
ocean, and the soft sheen of rich black that made a pailful
of them look like something Aladdin's djinn had djumped
ten thousand miles to fetch. Some of us took a skiff and
rowed across the harbor to spend a day, picnic and all,
filling our milk pails. We'd have all we could eat for
supper at home, and while Father and we children sat
around and felt good about everything, Mother stewed up
the rest and sealed them in pint jars for winter. A winter
breakfast with wild blackcap jam on hot sal'ratus biscuits
was one of the privileges of living at our house, and is an
advantage I'm glad for. I never had a shiny new bicycle,
and I've never had bank deposits. But I've had blackcap
jam on hot biscuits, and my boyhood was rich. Frank
Blaisdell used to come down and pick with us, too. He
never said anything about picking his blackcaps. Wild
raspberries may not have a legalized status, or they may
have—but we knew they were in the public domain, and
so did Frank.

So what happened? One day a rich New Yorker came
to our town, one of the early crop of vacationists, and he
bought the whole point. Paid a good price, Frank said, and
then he put a fence around it. Woven wire with metal
posts. Cost a fortune. He not only fenced people out
across the neck, but he fenced himself in around the water.
Did it up right. People around town were interested, but
they didn't mind, because we understood how it is with
people who never had ownership of land in their back-
grounds. The poor man had a deep sense of possession.

He'd slaved away a whole lifetime at something he hated, so he could retire to Maine and own some land, and when he got it he naturally put up a fence so he could walk around and see just what was his. People in our town wouldn't have done anything like that, themselves. But they could see how it was. Our people have always been land poor. That's an expression. You're land poor when you've got more land than you can work. A fence, to us, was something you put up to keep your cows in, or to keep other cows out, and it was hardly ever looked upon as a barrier. We never had a line fence spat that I remember, except the time Elliott Dineen found old Charlie Dennison had set a fence about fifteen feet over the line. Charlie didn't know Elliott cared, it just so happened that it was easier to put the fence where it was, than where it should be. So Charlie went over with a crowbar, and he said to Elliott, "You take this, and you put it where you please, and we'll make that the line—that swamp in there ain't worth ten cents a county, and you know it as well as I do." That was the end of that, and the only other fence dispute we ever had was the lingering war between Deacon Justin Maybury and Pushpin Taylor, and that wasn't really over a fence at all. Deacon came home from prayer meeting a little ahead of time one night, and caught Pushpin climbing out of his bedroom window, at which the deacon's wife showed a great deal of surprise and dismay. The fence dispute was just an excuse, but the Deacon kept picking on Pushpin after that over the fence, and his wife always attended prayer meeting with him. Otherwise we never had much exhibition of concern over who owned what.

But after this New Yorker fenced off Blaisdell's Point, people called it The Bowery. It is a tedious kind of humor, but it hit the nail on the head, and it has been called The Bowery ever since. It shows, I suppose, how a

State of Mainer feels about the ownership of real estate. The fence didn't bother much at first. When the blackcaps were ripe, we went down and climbed over the fence and picked them. There was a big oak tree in one corner, with a limb that hung just so, and we could swing over the fence pails and all. But after a few days the New Yorker put up a sign that said No Trespassing Under Penalty Of The Law, and cut off the limb. Under Maine law, which isn't altogether satisfactory in all respects, I think you sue for trespass, which is very different from having somebody arrested. Those of us who climbed the fence after that were threatened with arrest. It is a curious thing to be an unfettered Maine boy doing nothing any more wicked than picking yourself a few wild raspberries, and having a deep voice come to you from afar which says, "Get out of there or I'll call the police!" I'm afraid the New Yorker overestimated our opinion of the police. The only police we knew anything about was Lester Newcomb, and he was only a constable. He also had duties as humane officer, and once in a while spoke to people who abused their animals. As constable of the town, his outstanding act of service was to post the warrants for Town Meeting, and if he ever arrested anybody it happened without my knowing it. We had a deputy sheriff in town, too, but sometimes the older men would dispute amongst themselves as to who it was this year. Anyway, we were greatly puzzled by the state of affairs, and rowed back across the harbor discussing whether or not a man could kick you off his property. It was a strange thing to have happen. We had been evicted from an inalienable right. Mother told me the man was queer, and that took care of the whole thing. After that we only picked blackcaps when he wasn't around. Otherwise, the blackcaps ripened in the sun as before, but they dropped off the bushes when they were ripe, and the New Yorker walked about his woven wire fence and basked in the importance of ownership.

A few years later this New Yorker felt the road out to his place wasn't just what he'd like. A thousand years before, the Indians had come across-lots from somewhere up-country, and they had gone out onto The Bowery to eat clams and lobsters. The shell heaps were big. Indian trails are fine if you walk, and accommodate your step beautifully to the lay of the land. But they make poor roads for low-slung vehicles. In the colonial days a few of the bends had been straightened, making it easier to take hides and lumber and crops to the wharf, but for the most part the road to The Bowery was the same road that prevailed when the Paint People first went down there to find food. At just about the time public indignation over the blackcaps was highest, the New Yorker met Arthur Mercennes, our road commissioner, and said he thought it would be nice to have a new road out to the point. Art said it was a splendid idea, that he thought a five- or six-lane job done with solid gold paving blocks and diamond-studded culverts would be a great improvement, and he supposed a good many people would volunteer to work on it for nothing except the glory. One word led to another, and Art finally punched the New Yorker in the nose.

The New Yorker brought suit, but when he found out so many people were clamoring to be on the jury, he dropped it. Then he made a political issue of it, and began to work hard to get Art beaten the next year at Town Meeting. Art liked that, and said he couldn't think of anybody he'd rather have opposing him. The New Yorker also put an article in the Town Warrant asking for $5,000 to construct a passable road to his point. Art figured it up, and said that all the money ever spent on that road, including what the Indians did, had been under $700. Art said the proposed road could only serve two possible purposes—either to take people out to the point to see the New Yorker, which nobody would want to do; or bring the New Yorker to town, which he thought was entirely unnecessary. The article in the warrant was dismissed, which means the Town refused to consider it, and Art was reelected by the biggest majority he ever got. I say "majority," because I have to say something—nobody ever ran against Art, and consequently there wasn't too much need of voting for him. He would go in if he just voted for himself. But that year everybody voted for him.

The truth was that Art couldn't build a road in a sand box. He always said the most important thing for a road commissioner to know was how to get elected. Then he would hire an engineer to do the work. If the engineer didn't do a good job, Art could fire him, but once Art was elected, it was his show. We always had good roads, except down to The Bowery.

The next year this New Yorker decided he would offer his services to the Town and be a member of the school board. He said the schools needed improving, and he was willing to give his time. He was particularly fitted for the job, had a good education and had done fine in business. But Art was opposed to it. He said something about people who had lived in town 24 hours trying to run everything. A lot of people said it was too bad not to vote for him, because he was such an able man, but nobody did. In fact, they didn't get a chance to, because Art Mercennes prevailed on one of our village halfwits to run for the school board, and a contest developed. The question came up—was it worse to defeat a halfwit, or worse to be beaten by one? The New Yorker saw the point, and withdrew. So Art had the halfwit withdraw, and at the last minute he said he would run in the absence of another candidate, and Art was both road commissioner and school committeeman for a long time. The New

Yorker has never played a prominent part in local affairs.

Art was one who seldom missed a chance. He died not long ago. Addie Prout met my mother on the street, and Addie said, "Arthur Mercennes died!"

Mother said, "No!"

Addie said, "Yes, they found him dead in bed."

And Mother said, "Whose bed?"

But it's funny how those things hold over. In late years a lot of people have built cottages and homes down along the Blaisdell Point road, and some of them are nice people. But the road has never been repaired, and as long as that fence stands around the blackcap raspberries, I doubt if it ever will be. The thing about Art was that he knew what blackcaps meant to our town. Break it down, and he knew what they meant, and mean, to me. He wasn't just a road commissioner. He was a good old soul who was born and brought up in the house his great-grandfather built, and he lived life as he found it in our town. He knew the town, and he knew all these people in it. And they knew him.

And I guess that life in a small town like mine has a lot more to do with tide-sweetened blackcap raspberries than it has with reason and logic and persuasion, and things like that. And I think that's a good idea.

Saunders

THE first game I ever shot was a long-haired pussy cat named Albert, and I got him with a bow and arrow. Boys in my town learned to shoot before they were very old, and it wasn't always a gun that we preferred. This pussy cat owed his untimely demise to the fact that my uncle had been "out west" when they opened up the country and, I gather, used his key. He made me a bow and taught me to use it, and this was back quite a time before the current sporty interest in archery. The cat was a chicken stealer and a successful minor operation in his youth had produced unusual growth, until he was as big as four cats without counting his long hair. My father saw him climbing over the fence of the chicken pen one day with a recently deceased chicken in his mouth, and my father was awful mad.

The cat belonged to Mrs. Stevens, the kindly widow of a Captain Stevens who had originally brought the particular strain of Stevens cat to this country from, probably,

Persia. Mrs. Stevens had numerous cats, but Albert was most magnificent, and there was nothing else like him anywhere, ever. My father, on successive days, saw Albert going home with other chickens, and he reflected that if this kept up any length of time, our flock of chickens would be extremely small, and Albert might put on so much weight that Mrs. Stevens would hold a grudge against us for over-feeding her Albert. So my father loaded his shotgun and went out and stalked Albert, and presently he was rewarded by the sight of Albert, chick in mouth, climbing the fence post in such a way that he elevated himself directly into the sight of the shotgun. My father was about to salute him when Mrs. Stevens stood up in the bushes down behind her house, where she was picking raspberries, and she called, "Don't you shoot Albert!"

Father heard her, and assuming that she meant the particular Albert he was about to shoot, he felt neighborhood harmony would be more salutary if he didn't squeeze the trigger at that time. He waved the gun around and broke the breech as if he were hefting the gun to see if he liked it, and after Albert had gone home he came in the house and delivered a stirring lecture on the subject of the Widow Stevens and her illegitimate cat. The situation was aggravated by the knowledge that Mrs. Stevens knew her cat was stealing chickens, and that she would not take any steps to keep him home, break him of the habit, or say she was sorry. Sea captains' widows often were like that. My father figured a day would come when she would be otherwise, and her cat would not. If the chickens held out.

Coping with Albert gave me an opportunity to acquire skill in the use of the bow. It was not the longbow this time, it was the short buffalo-hunting bow of the Sioux Nation, and my Sioux Shooting Uncle made it from a spruce limb. I think spruce is not often considered ideal bow timber, but there is nothing better. When a long, overhanging spruce limb has died on the tree and has dried hanging up, it has a natural curve in it, and can be tapered off with a small plane and a piece of broken glass. It grows tougher as it gets older. Uncle tapered it, stroking it gently with the broken glass, and meditating as a man will when he is working a piece of good wood. He got down the old spinning wheel, and with some linen ends from the shoe shop he spun a bowstring with great care that I should observe the principle, and know how to make one for myself if necessity arose. Then he made the arrow. It was from a pine boat-board, as straight as any shortest distance between two points, and he fitted one end with a knife blade. I turned the hand emery wheel for him while he shaped it, dipping it into a can of water to keep the temper, and rounding it so both edges were alike and keen as razors. He used gull wingfeathers on the other end, setting them with glue. And this whole industry took only a forenoon and part of the after-dinner, so by evening we were out practicing.

Uncle had some old playing cards, and he would lay one against the manure pile and I would shoot at it. He showed me how to hold the string, and how to pull. And when I let go, the arrow went into the manure pile and didn't hurt anything. Uncle would walk over and get the arrow, and bring it back and tell me to try again. It didn't take long, and although my shooting fingers got sore, the next day found me a reasonably proficient Sioux sannup, and I was clipping the card as often as not. Uncle said that with practice I could hit the card as often as a man with a rifle, at that distance, but I think he was wrong —within two days I could hit it better. And then he pointed out Albert to me, for Albert was coming up over the fence post with another chicken.

The lethal quality of a bow is scarcely understood by a lot of people. They read of the battles of Agincourt and Hastings, and make historical note of the fact that bows were used, but I think they dismiss them except that they may have a nuisance value. The picture may be changed somewhat since the colleges have permitted young women to major in archery, but in my time I have definitely found a public tendency to dismiss a bow as a plaything. Albert could have said different. Albert was pinned to that post so that he had nothing to do but go around and around like a pinwheel, and while he was doing it my uncle ran up and hit him with a shovel, and I never heard of Albert's stealing chickens again. The bow, certainly, proved that it can take game without making a loud report, and the kindly Widow Stevens never knew that Albert had been done in. She may have suspected it, but under the law that was her privilege.

After that Uncle made me some blunt arrows to play with, and I kept the sharp one for hunting. It did get some rabbits now and then, and several crows. The blunt arrows would take woodchucks, and we got rafts of them. We used to shoot rats with bows, and we shot at a good many other things. When I exhibited my Indian bow around, some of the boys immediately showed up with other types. One boy had a real English longbow with a plush handle and horn tips for the string. A crossbow came next, and one lad had an uncle whose range of knowledge included a real blowgun with wicked little darts. The darts weren't sharp, but they had a wallop to them that would make a horse run quite a way, and the boy had his blowgun taken from him when they caught him blowing at passing buggies. Somehow, as we grew up, we were given the idea that weapons were for game, and should never be aimed at anything you didn't want to hit. We also had skill enough with our various weapons to realize that a weapon will hit what it's aimed at. None of us ever got shot.

Later on we all had .22 rifles, and by the time we were in high school we had leave to do some real hunting with deer rifles and shotguns. But Teddy Linell, one of my brave warriors, used to go shooting with his bow when he was a grown man. I have myself, but I didn't hit anything. He used to get game. When he was in high school he took a rich uncle from the city out after ducks and geese, and the rich uncle thoughtlessly made some joshing remarks about "Locksley," and the good sheriff of Nottinghamshire, and so on and so forth. But Teddy knew what he was doing. There was a law against shooting geese with a rifle, which is a good law, because usually they will sit on the water just out of reach of double-B's, and a rifle might carry to them if a good man aimed it. But Teddy's bow had no legal status under the game laws, even though he could give it rifle fidelity for an amazing distance. He got three geese, each neatly spitted on an arrow, and his uncle didn't get anything.

With the bow in my background that way, I've often thought Maine should adopt them for all hunting, at least for all rifle hunting. Some effort has been made toward that by archery enthusiasts, but the great intellectuals in our law-making body have ridiculed the idea. I guess none of them ever heard of Agincourt, because they get up and make remarks about cowboys and Indians, and in effect suggest that the archers go home and stop being silly. All I know is that every fall we have a lot of dead men to lug out of the woods, sometimes almost as many as we have deer, and I think I would rather play cowboy and Indian than be sent home to a sorrowing widow. I imagine the people who sell firearms and ammunition are opposed to the idea, and some of the legislators may have been in contact with them, but in any event, bows don't enjoy legislative approval. A bow will perforate a Montgomery-Ward catalog from quite a distance, and shouldn't restrict the gunner as much as he imagines. He would have to learn to use it, though. This would hamper him, because he can go shooting deer with a rifle now without being obliged to know how to use it. A gun has a way of going off by itself, something a bow doesn't do because of its nature. Sometimes a man with an automatic rifle will stand in a palsied trance and shoot the chamber empty at his own mother and not know he did it. Mothers have a way of looking like a deer to a lot of stalwart hunters who have matriculated with the very best sporting goods stores, and been graduated summa cum laude in a red hat. I think a bow in their hands would be a great social improvement. And on top of everything else, it would make the fall woods a good deal quieter, and we wouldn't have to listen to the present bombardment.

Weapons, however, were not a primary matter. We took them to the woods with us, but the important thing was that we went to the woods. We went to the woods in all weather and all seasons, and there wasn't much we didn't know about them. The woods of Maine are a fine thing to have in your background, and although our boyhood in them was fun, there were plenty of grim realities that pointed up our play into great educational advantages.

One of the grimmest of realities came one day when my particular crowd of scouts invited a very ladylike playmate to go on a trip with us. He had never joined in our kind of play, partly because his mother was a dressmaker and his father had gone away to be alone, and the boy didn't have a very good bringing up. He was a sissy. We all felt sorry for him, we really did, and we tried to find some way to fit him in. We asked him to go, and while we packed the sacks he was sent to the store to buy the steak. We pooled our funds, and Patsy, as we called him, was to make the purchase. He came back from the store shortly, and we stuck the bundle in a packsack, and away we went o'er hill and dale and came presently to our spring of water and our campsite. It was just dusk, we were miles from home, and supper sounded like a magnificent idea. We got the bed of coals ready, and unwrapped the steak.

Well, Patsy hadn't bought steak. He had bought a bag of dates and figs. I think it is understandable. I guess that his diet had never included dates and figs, and he had always wanted some. Having funds at hand, and seeing dates and figs available, he had yielded to an urge. And not knowing much about long treks through the hunger-charging wilderness, he hadn't realized how inappropriate dates and figs would look at supper time. The moment was indeed grim, and we Daniel Boones stared down at the opened bag. Give us credit, though, we were gentlemen. We excused ourselves, and said none of us cared for fruit, and we ate the fried potatoes and drank the fragrant nectar of the coffee bean, and chewed on our biscuits, and allowed Patsy to eat his fill of dates and figs. Then we laid down upon our fir beds and nursed our consuming hunger all night, and got up and went home. Patsy complained during the night of gastronomic inquietude, but he was all right by daylight, and we always looked at our groceries before we started out on subsequent trips.

There were, though, moments that seemed less grim, but might have been worse. One time a half dozen of us crept from a watery grave when a raft tipped up, and all of us had dry matches for a fire. My training never included the ability to rub sticks together to make flame. It was considered much more satisfactory to strike a match. Our training called for keeping the matches dry. We had glass bottles stoppered with sealing wax, and we had matches dipped in wax. We learned to put the matches in the bottle head first, so we could get them out with wet fingers and still have them light. We were taught that a damp match would light if you rubbed it first in your hair. And we knew how to get kindlings when it had been raining for days. We could go into the woods wet and come out dry, and sometimes did. It is a fine thing to know that you can set up a camp, make a fire, cook a supper, and sleep dry as a bone while a rainstorm is raging and the woods are dripping the way they drip on a stormy night.

The Maine woods have no animals or reptiles that will hurt you. All the time I've lived in Maine, I've never seen a bear in the woods, and very few people have. I've seen them in traps, ready to be taken, and I've seen them hanging with one foot badly mangled while some mighty hunter related how many shots it took to get him. The bear is nocturnal in habit, and very shy. He will put up a scrap if cornered, but so will a house mouse. A black bear is seldom cornered except by accident, and it is fear that throws him into gear. He can outrun almost anything, and if you let him alone he will disappear before your eyes. He usually disappears before anybody sees him, and I imagine the only times hunters really come upon them with opportunity to shoot is when the bear is busy eating, or sometimes when the hungry bear is sneaking up on your bacon and butter in camp, and you snap a flashlight to see what that noise is. A porcupine will make the same noise, and upon running away will make a good deal more than a bear. I suspect many a bear that got away was really a porcupine. Aside from a bear, there isn't anything I know of in the Maine woods that will cause alarm, not counting the man-eating trout of Gogalog Bog, who wear neckties and play the banjo, and always tip their hats before they chase you. I have never seen one myself, but many people have, and Jim Berry said when he climbed a tree they jumped up and down on the ground snapping at his heels. At least we boys never saw anything to frighten us, and we certainly gave the woods every chance to do so.

The only real danger in the woods, and I imagine this goes for woods anywhere, is the fear that is said to come over people who get lost. I never got lost, and I've never known anybody except babies who did, so I don't know, but certainly the things some lost hunters do show they are beset with an intense and reason-killing fear. They run wildly through the trees at night and shout and waste their strength. Our older folks taught us there was one and only one remedy for getting lost. It was to find a rock or a stump or a log, and sit down on it and stay there. Sometimes staying there would gradually restore faith in your own ability, and you'd get up and go home. But if you were really lost, you would be there, and would be alive and well when people came to find you. Some of the modern sportsmen have signals they perform with their rifles if they get lost, but our training called for a simpler signal that can be used by people without guns. It was to get a stick, which can always be found somewhere in the woods, and to take it up and pound the be-jabbers out of a tree. This makes quite a racket, and can be heard by searchers, and doesn't call for loud shouting. Loud shouting tends to increase your fear, they say, because it comes back at you and makes you lonely. Besides, belting a tree with a stick amuses you, because you can see how much bark you are pounding off, and it also gives you warming exercise if the night be cold. I never did it, so I don't know, but I do know that any of my crowd would do it rather than spend the night wandering and running. You can't always tell, of course, what a person will do when the emergency finally comes, but at least our folks tried to give us a good grounding, and after that it was up to us.

Once in one of our projects, we decided to see how long it would take to make a shellheap. We learned, that way, how to cook seaside picnics, and that was one thing, but we also learned it takes a long time to make a shellheap. The end of the point, where the Indians had dumped clams all those years, attracted us—first, we dug out relics. We had some good ones. I still have some arrow heads around. Once a professor came and asked us to show him our relics, and we did, and then he asked us where we got them. We led him quite a chase before he tumbled that we were protecting our secret. But we did hold regular clambakes, by appointment, at the same place for several summers, and we dumped our picnic stuff always in the same spot so we could see how big the pile got. The foxes and skunks raked it over between picnics, and after a while we concluded that shellheaps take more time than we'd ever have. A few years ago I went back to the place, and there was no remnant of our feasts. Whatever we contributed to the ageless history of clambakes had mingled with the eons past. Perhaps in eons yet to come, long after our coastal shelf has gone beneath the waves and risen again, some peering professor will comb the heap, and if he finds a broken mustard jar, that will be me. What he won't find is the pleasure and satisfaction that we had, as boys, squatting there by the tide pursuing our scientific research. He won't know how much it meant to us as we arose, glutted, and made our ways out into the world. I never go by an expensive city playground, but I feel sorry for the children who can't explore shellheaps.

We changed with the seasons. In the fall we trapped skunks. Once I caught one under the banking boards on the back of the house, right under Mother's pantry window, and Mother was not inclined to hilarity. She moved to the parlor presently. We shot with a bright-speaking shotgun and murdered the skunk with such instantaneous dispatch that a good part of him was never found, but we weren't quick enough to frustrate his biological functions. He was gone but not forgotten. A skunk is easy to catch, if anyone wants to, and their skins sometimes bring amazing prices. I got $4.50 for one skin once, and this prompted a great wave of skunk catching, but the market collapsed and everybody was stuck with a bale of pelts worth about 25¢ each. At 25¢, the skunk is not considered such an asset as he is at $4.50. The $4.50 pleased me, and I was rich.

A dead hen makes a good excuse to catch a skunk. You plant the hen in some unfrequented place, and after a night or two you will see where a skunk has been digging for her. Then you set a trap, and the next morning you go to school smelling very loud. One time we detached certain portions of the anatomy of a large and vociferous skunk, and presented him to our teacher. She didn't know we had made this presentation, because she hadn't opened her desk drawer yet, and as the odor of skunk wafting in our school room was nothing unusual, she made no comments of gratitude. When she did, however, she slammed her drawer shut and called out, "Who's been trapping skunks?" Roscoe Purington, who did not know that some of us had honored the teacher in this way, but who had that very morning caught a splendid skunk in his henhouse, honestly and innocently raised his hand, whereupon the teacher gave him an awful licking. When she got through she gave him another one, and Roscoe was bewildered at this unexpected display of animosity. But at recess he found out what the score was, and he licked the whole bunch of us. We stood up and let him. We were laughing so hard it didn't hurt, and we didn't mind.

Our teacher was allergic to skunks, and she didn't come back after the Christmas vacation.

It is also possible to take skunks without fouling the neighborhood. You go out at night with a lantern, and you find a skunk prowling around, and you wait until he begins to run. When he begins to run, you hit him as tite as you can jump with a club, and he will lie down and behave himself. You must not, however, hit him when he is standing still, as that offends him deeply, and he will make you wish you hadn't. I do not know why this is so, but our older folks told us it was because a skunk in motion has thrown his anatomy out of gear. He is in neutral, sort of. And that is a good way for a skunk to be. Somehow I am amused as I think back, and recollect our skunk business. It gave us real money, sometimes, and while we no doubt contributed much to our poise and culture by the business, it must have made us obnoxious around about. But skunks were in the program, and we caught skunks, and there was more than one kind of value there.

Box traps were fun, too. We liked squirrels best, and we all had wire cages with exercising wheels. Once I brought home a new squirrel, and while everybody stood around and watched, I dumped him in the cage out of the box trap, and he turned out to be a rabbit. This amused everybody but me and the rabbit, and I think he was ashamed. We also set snares for rabbits, and caught many a hound dog. Once we took up hawking. Somebody had read a book, and hawking was at once the style. We set steel traps on poles near the hen ranges, and soon had hawks enough. One of my pals has a crooked ear to this day, and I can hear him yelling yet as the hawk tried to pull it out of his head. After a few days some older person told us we should really have a fledgling hawk for training, but we didn't know where to get one and the sport lapsed again into antiquity. I remember my pal, with his ear streaming blood, wrung the hawk's neck and threw him away, and then the hawk jumped up and flew to a far place. I wouldn't any more think of trying to catch and tame a white-tailed hawk today than I would think of singing soprano for an opera, but there it was in my boyhood, and we made out.

The thing was, that all these various escapades and adventures kept us in the open, and gave us something to do and taught us the ways of Nature—and the ways of people. Some of the things turned into money-makers when we picked berries to sell, or cut Christmas trees, or chopped wood, or even gathered juniper berries for intemperate old sea captains who believed they could make a better gin than the kinds currently on the market. Once the whole bunch of us picked blackberries for a captain who wanted to make some cordial, and if you are interested, it takes twenty-three bushels to make his recipe. You have to know the woods to find that many. So we grew up, and the woods of Maine were in our background, and there are people in this world who would say that's a good thing.

THE post-card notice for a Grange meeting gave the date and time, and was always concluded with the sentence, "All those not solicited please bring cake." All those not solicited thereupon brought cake, and the growing boy in my town learned that life can be beautiful. Those who had been solicited by the supper committee brought the baked beans, the cold ham, the potatoes, the pickles and cream, and the pies. But all those not solicited greatly outnumbered the special donors, and the cake display at a Grange supper is something nobody ever stared down.

Not long ago the Maine Development Commission, which is an expensive department in our frustrated state government, decided it would do a little work, and it announced that an effort would be made to rewrite the good old Maine recipes and standardize the dimensions and quantities. This was eminently humorous to folks who had ever dealt with a Maine recipe, which is first of all a contradiction in terms. Maine, as a connotative adjective, implies individuality and don't-give-a-cuss, while the word recipe would suggest a somewhat tabulated collection of recognizable facts. A Maine recipe, however, has never been anything you could go by, and a Maine housewife used them only to give her a general idea of the way things looked. Starting with that general idea, a woman could safely say, "I am baking a pie," although if pressed for recapitulative details she might not be able to tell you what kind or how many. When a Maine housewife says she "takes a little butter" there is no human capacity for understanding that can detach that phrase from the woman's own intentions. Other women can take a little butter, too, and no mortal judgment will be able to tell which of them happened on the correct amount—because there is no correct amount, and tabulation is absurd, and all of them are right. "A handful of salt" naturally depends on how big a hand you are talking about, and to reduce that to terms of ounces or tablespoons or cups is to remove from the picture all the processes of reason, discernment and judgment that make a woman a cook. The project of our state department, I could see, was a step in the wrong direction. What we need is women who know how much sugar to use, whether the recipe tells them how much or not, and until that era runs around again I shall continue to view my boyhood as remarkable.

It was that way with Grange supper cakes. Not one of them was ever manufactured from an immutable receet, and no two were ever alike, nor was any one of them alike twice. I have baked many a fine cake myself, and I wouldn't wonder if I may bake another one or two soon, and I know. You take some of this and some of that, and as you go along you keep thinking up wonderful things to do, and instead of the simple cottage sponge you had in mind when you broke the first egg, you may end up with a magnificent structure that looks more like the Taj Mahal, or the golden scenes of the eternal Zion, than something to eat. If you have a receet and insist on its changeless sameness, you will always wind up with the same old cake, and that will cause a lot of worry among your relatives and friends who are wondering if you have lost your touch. Grange supper cakes were not a part of the regular baking. They were baked along in the afternoon, usually, in a separate rite all by themselves. "I'm going to bake the cake now," Mother would say. She said this partly to warn us that we must not slam doors and run in the house, because superstition has it that undue commotion would make the cake "fall." My mother never had a cake fall, and I have seen very few that ever did. Once Mrs. Thelma Brawn was baking a big thick cake that was supposed to be susceptible to falling, and she neglected to speak about her intentions, and while it was baking she went upstairs to comb her hair. Her brother didn't know about the cake, so he came into the kitchen with an ash log and an ax, and he hewed out a pair of oars right by the stove, and when Thelma came down she nearly fainted at the noise and concussion. But the cake didn't fall. So in fifty or seventy-five homes in town cakes would be baked the afternoon of Grange, and in the evening everybody would go to Grange with his cake on an inverted platter, and comparisons would run around while everybody decided which one he liked the looks of best.

Now the women knew this comparison business was coming, and they made ready for it. Each one put her best foot forward. Ingenuity flowered into great bouquets, and every woman who competed had been almost maliciously determined. You would naturally suppose that a woman who frosted a double-decker and studded the top with butternuts and candied quince would stand some chance of becoming famous. But that would be the night Mrs. Wallace would decide to show off, and Mrs. Wallace

41

would bring a simple cottage cake about six inches high with no frosting at all. Mrs. Wallace would also bring a bowl and an egg beater, a jar of heavy cream and a basket of peaches, and after she got there she would whip the cream, cover the cake, and stud it with halves of fresh peaches in such a way that Benvenuto Cellini would have taken one look and put his eyes out. You can't whip cream too long before eating time, and you can't bring a creamed cake any distance, so Mrs. Wallace didn't intend to take a back seat and she finished the job on the spot. Competition was severe.

But beauty is only skin deep, and less pretentious cakes had merit too. I discovered once that the best cake that ever came to Grange was far from being a thing of beauty, and looked so inferior that the supper committee seldom served it, but saved it for the cake auction after the meeting, when uneaten food was bid for. A little woman from Palmer Point made it, a fisherman's wife whose stringy gray hair was always drawn back into a pug with such vicious tightness that she always stared and couldn't get her eyes shut. Her waterside home was neat, but small and remote. Nobody knew much about her and her husband, and we saw them only at Grange. They came by boat, and would sit all evening by themselves and not talk. Fisher-people sometimes get like that. There is a kind of communion of perceptions for them, and they have no need of talk. After the meeting they would walk down to the Town Landing and row out into the night and go home. The cake she baked was looked upon, I'm afraid, as a well-meant donation that the committee must receive with some show of appreciation. But one night I had a piece of it at my end of the table, and I found that God had lavished a great gift on one of His lesser children. Boy fashion, I asked the woman for her receet, because I frequently tried my mother's own self-esteem by bringing home receets for her to work on. But the little woman from Palmer Point didn't have a receet, and she did her best to explain how the cake was made. There was coffee in the cake—and it was the real coastal mug-up coffee that could stand in a gale and blow a foghorn if anybody asked it to. But the batter had island cranberries in it, and streaks of something like marshmallow, and all the most incongruous-sounding ideas that nobody but a sheer kitchen genius would ever have attempted. No rational thinking process would ever have deduced that such-and-such a series of premises would arrive at a palatable conclusion. It sounded as if the little woman was making up things to delude anybody who would try to imitate her masterpiece. But that wasn't so—the cake really had those things in it, and it was a chewy kind of cake, one you could linger on and mull over, and for many a Grange supper after that I would hunt for that cake and eat the most of it alone. But I didn't know enough to keep my big mouth shut, and one by one the other children learned my secret, and soon came a Grange supper when I didn't get any of it at all, and word went around that the little lady from Palmer Point baked a nice cake. Even Mrs. Wallace asked her for the receet and tried to bake such a cake, but she couldn't get it right. My mother tried it, and it didn't taste the same. I think, really, my discovery brought a certain amount of unhappiness to the little tight-haired woman, because after that the women used to speak to her, and tried to make talk with her, and she had to try to talk back when she preferred to sit there with her husband and commune. But she did bake one of the finest cakes I ever tasted—even though it looked most unlikely as it sat on the Grange cake table amongst the select and well-dressed offerings of our more artistic members.

Frosting seems to be a deceiver, therefore, and should

not be relied on wholly, because this woman's cake had no frosting on it. It had brown paper around it, and seemed to have little warts where the cranberries were. Aside from looks, there were no bad cakes at Grange. The quantity of cakes caused confusion, and judgment had to be visual until adequate sampling could be done. Some seemed to be better than others, which was an optical illusion. Thus I was taught not to jump at conclusions, and that is a very good thing to know. A boy will find that he should sample all the cakes because cakes were never baked to look at, and he will find that it sometimes takes several pieces of each to deduce adequate distinctions and arrive at a competent decision. He will grow up, then, with unbiased powers of circumspection, and will not often be fooled. I would urge all parents to let their children attend Grange suppers, if they can find one such as we used to have, and allow them to practice discernment until they have secured an adequate quantity of it. It will be helpful, and in later life will bear rich and beautiful rewards.

Something like the cake table at Grange supper was the food sale. A food sale was supposed to be a public market at which the church or some woman's group sought to pick up some funds for their treasuries. Each woman donated some article of cooked food, and as with the cakes at Grange, much vying took place. The theory of a public market bogged down in practice, though, and the food sale was completely doctored. Unless you had the right connections you could starve to death before you could buy anything.

It worked this way: After the decision was made to hold a food sale, the women would make arrangements among themselves, and they would decide which woman was going to be permitted to buy which woman's wares. It was well known that every cook had a specialty. With my mother it was a toss-up between doughnuts and apple pie, although this was just popular fancy because my mother could cook circles around the whole town and not half try on anything edible. But this dickering went on, and by the time the sale was due to open nearly everything was already bargained for and sometimes paid for, and the boxes were marked and kept under the table.

The vestry of the church was the favorite food sale location. If in later days you happened to be a tourist and saw the sign, "Food Sale Today," you would go in and find out that the front entry of our church smelled just the same as the front entry of a church anywhere else. If I am ever rich, I am going to install ventilators on that church and see if the 1872 air can't be brought up to date. Doctrines differ, but the must and dust of church vestibules knows not creed or cult. But as you pass through the vestibule and into the vestry, you will find that the food sale has done something to the atmosphere. The left-over wrath of God has taken on the aroma of spiced cookies and molasses brownbread and punkin pies and jelly rolls and hot new bread, and while this is overwhelming in its totality, it is still distinctive in its components. You may smell mince turnovers if you choose to smell mince turnovers, or you can take a more comprehensive whiff and get everything at once. There was a time I supposed the church entry was purposely stagnant to enhance the food sale when you came to it, but that is expecting too much. The only other time there was any enhancing was at Christmastree time, when the entry's gospel air of dead yesterdays accented the vestry's evergreen and popcorn gayety. It always seemed wrong to me to make Santa Claus wait in that gloom, with the recollection of bygones hanging suspended in the air, while the expectant children completed the recitation program.

But now that you are in the vestry you will see the

people. Five is a good number for a committee, and five women will therefore be sitting behind the table with an entertaining array of hats, all talking at once. A few other women will be present and will be permitted to talk, but not being members of the committee they must do it discreetly around the edges of the room. But what will amaze you most is the great scarcity of food. The table is far from cluttered. You will see a wan pink and yellow cake, a dozen hermit cookies, a small plate of macaroons, and an assortment of fudges which are to be sold at a cent a bite. It was possible to buy fudge in quantity, but this was done so seldom that nobody ever figured out a price in terms of ounces and pounds. Most of the fudge will be bought by the committee and those in the corners of the vestry, and consumed on the spot.

It seems impossible that this slight and disappointing array of food could transform the vestry atmosphere into the delicious moment now met. It is more than a run-of-the-mill religious miracle. If you are not too overcome by the enigma, you may decide to buy a few pieces of fudge and make a graceful exit. Perhaps you will take the macaroons. But the pink and yellow cake has no appeal. That is because the pink and yellow cake was purposely made to resist buying, so the committee would still have something to display at closing time. That is a ridiculous statement, and I make it with full realization that it will be denied—but in my town a sickly pink and yellow cake could have been cooked only by design. I know that.

But while you are sampling the fudge, and trying to figure out what is making all this magnificent aroma of cooked food, in will come, say, Mary Warren, and she will carry on a spirited conversation simultaneously with all the women in sight, and she will peel out a dollar bill and say she has come for her pie. Then one of the women on the committee will get up and stoop over, and from under the table she will produce a mince pie about the size of a bicycle wheel, and it will be all golden brown around the edges, and will smell like something the gods wish they could match, and there will still be a trace of steam coming out of the little cuts in the crust, and the woman will tie it up so Mary can take it home and start supper. If you hang around you will find that other women will come in, and each of them will get something from under the table, and if you stay long enough you will find that the ladies will sell food all afternoon and do a rushing business, and nobody will buy anything from the slight assortment that was there when you came in. Such is a food sale, and they made my father awful mad.

"You spend a dollar to mix and fry doughnuts, and give them away, and then you buy something for a dollar and bring it home for us to eat, and I'd-a damn sight rather have your doughnuts." Father would say a food sale meant he got milked for two dollars, and he had to eat somebody's else idea of food. Mother would smile and say it was in a good cause, and if Mother said so, I guess it was.

But the food sale and the Grange supper gave us boys a chance to see the infinite variety of food that could be manufactured amongst our women, and it gave us ideas about planning a home of our own. Consequently, I'm sure, each of us exercised great caution in selecting a wife, and has not been fooled over much by the more modern contentions that recipes have something to do with cooking. Food is a fact of life, and we learned about it where it grew. Trying to standardize the old Maine receets is silly. What they ought to do is teach the Grange supper and the Ladies' Circle food sale in school today, just as they do any other social science.

SOME of our characters were better characters than others, and I suppose I'd better go into that so people won't think we were all more or less normal, for us. Two of our best queer characters were special friends of mine, and there were plenty of others who were known to me, and who unquestionably left some kind of an impression. One of these special two was Mark Martin, who later came to be the Archbishop in St. Mark's Cathedral.

This particular St. Mark's Cathedral I speak of was nothing but Mark's woodshed, built over into a church, and this all came about after he began having visions. He let me view one of his visions with him once, but I didn't have the faith, although there's no question but he saw it, and saw it well. At the first of it Mark was a quiet and simple farmer up on Nubble Hill who saw through the magnificent wisdom of Mother Nature and allowed that creature to take care of him. He raised rabbits. Raising rabbits is not hard to do if you want to, since rabbits gestate in something like fifteen or twenty minutes, and the most necessary thing to have is something to do with them later.

Mark observed that wild rabbits, in the woods, are the victims of certain birds and animals, as well as man, who take them frequently from one end while the hardships of life continue to work on them from the other, as a result of which if they don't starve to death they are eaten. Mark figured that if he fenced in a good piece of his woodland, kept the predators out and provided shelter and food, the wild rabbits would tend to make him a wealthy man, in terms of rabbits. And since there was a fox farm in the next town which would buy rabbits to feed the foxes, Mark knew what he could do with all he raised. The fence he put up was tight and high, and he turned about two feet of it under ground so the rabbits wouldn't dig out and the dogs and foxes wouldn't dig in. Then he erected a number of poles with traps on them and figured he had controlled the hawks and owls. All he had to do was sit back and wait a few minutes.

When I was ten or twelve I used to go over to his place and sit and watch his rabbits. He had at least forty million of them, as near as anybody could tell, and they were racing around all day trying to step the figure up while there was yet time. He had a big net he would spring out over the feed whenever he wanted to catch some, and he'd get two or three dozen at a crack. He would pick out the ones ready to market, and leave his breeders. It was a great idea, and all Mark did was sit back and blow on a tin whistle to amuse himself. He kept a cow, but had no further investment in farming. His wife was dead; and his daughters had got married and had families, or vice versa, and Mark was enjoying himself in the quiet of his hilltop home with all his rabbits.

One day when I was over there Mark told me about his vision. He was coming out of the barn one morning with his milkpail full of new milk, and he chanced to look up in the sky and saw an angel going by, pushing a wheelbarrow full of stove wood. This astonished him somewhat, and occupied his attention rather completely. The angel nodded at him, and disappeared into a fissure in the sky. And while Mark was still looking, the fissure opened up and an angelic choir was discovered arranged like a symphony orchestra, with a big angel with a beard in the middle. This big angel turned and spoke to Mark and said, "The first number on the program will be *Abide with Me Fast Falls the Eventide.*" They sang it through, and then they sang a lot more hymns, and Mark thought it was all very pretty. He said the stage setting was very expensive, and must have cost a fortune, what with all manner of draperies and colors. The big angel asked Mark how he liked it, and Mark said it was first rate. So the big angel told Mark that he was Moses, and he had some instructions for Mark that came right from headquarters, and for Mark to rip out his woodshed and build a church. After he got that done, Moses said, he would receive further instructions. Later on that day Mark came to with a stiff neck from looking up in the sky so long, and he found the froth had all settled down on his pail of milk and the cream had risen and it was time to milk again. He had a partition all ripped out the day I was there, and showed me where he was going to have the ark of the convenant, and the pews, and the contribution box, and later on I heard that Mark had finished it up and was preaching every evening. Sometimes he'd have an audience, and sometimes he wouldn't, but he preached anyway. And then the news got around about the visions, and the whole thing became very popular. Almost everybody dropped around to see what was going on within the next few weeks, and they came away and said Mark was crazy as a coot.

I'm not sure he was. Everybody who came left some kind of a donation in the contribution box, and after a while Mark was able to use a very high priced whiskey for communion. Quite a congregation of horse jockeys, hired men, road workers and sundries would gather to assist in this ceremony, and some nights they'd make Mark repeat communion several times over until he got it just right. Somebody tried to get the deputy sheriff to put a stop to it, but he quoted the constitution, and said freedom of worship didn't exclude those who did it with strong drink, and as long as the Lord was a party to the thing the county would refrain from interference. So Mark prospered, and as time went along got a little band of faithful who took the whole thing seriously and were convinced that Mark was the real thing. Everybody else thought otherwise, but Mark didn't care.

His visions certainly weren't visible to anybody else, although he would stand there in the dooryard and point them out to you if you were there while he was having one. He had one one day when I was there. He said as time went along and the visions became more and more necessary because of the great deal of work he had to do, they settled down into two kinds. One was a quick, short vision intended to answer a minor problem. If Mark couldn't decide whether to go to town and recruit attendance, or stay home and prepare a sermon, he would go out and have a vision and see which way he was to act. But if some big problem came up, particularly a question of doctrine, the angels would stage quite a spectacle, with a big band and a lot of singing, and magic fire, and sometimes parades several miles long. People going by would see Mark out on the lawn looking up into the sky with his mouth open.

The truth was that Mark preached a good sermon. There was a lot of homespun truth in it, like pay your bills and look people in the eye, and don't neglect prayer, and take your problems to the Lord, and everything expounded in the language of the people. The particular people who formed his congregation came to be known as Holy Rollers, but that wasn't right, because we had Holy Rollers anyway. Some of the real Holy Rollers went over to him, partly because of his communion services, no doubt. But Mark's people didn't dance and jerk and roll around like the real Rollers. They were sedate and quiet, except on Communion nights when they got drunk. About the only difference this made was that they sang a lot of songs that weren't in the hymn book, and never will be, and used to make a lot of loud talk on the way home.

Mark had been a teamster in the woods in his youth, and had never cured himself of his teamster's language. His sermons and prayers were in keeping, and if the Good Lord ever inclined an ear to listen, He must have got singed. Mark gave our community a by-word, and it can still be heard in unrelated places and out of continuity, and will attest my remarks if you should doubt them. You ask anybody in town about "Amen, goddammit!" and he'll tell you about Mark Martin and his cathedral on Nubble Hill.

The other queer character I'm thinking of was our hermit. He built up a nice little business out of being a hermit, and after the summer tourists found out about him his business expanded so fast that he had to take on an assistant hermit. Our hermit lived in Whipsocket Hollow, a dip in the road that would excite your curiosity as you rode by. In the glacial days, we were told, chunks of ice got covered up with dirt, and ages long after they melted away and left those round holes in the ground. Maine has a lot of them. This one happened to lay where the road went, and made quite a dip. Down in the bottom was this little house, and the glacial gravel of the banks was insurance against the hole's filling with water. The hermit wasn't a hermit at first, he was just Roger Brewer who did carpenter work around by day, and whittled in his spare time. He was a real whittler, at first, one who doesn't make anything but just reduces a stick to shavings. Later he took to making things, and he used to have a little talk he'd give to folks who came in to watch him about the difference between a whittler and a wood carver. A whittler didn't have anything in mind. He was killing time, giving his hands some practice. But after Roger took up carving, he made a lot of nice things. He brought some of them down to the library once and put on an exhibit, and sat amongst the books and whittled until Miss Harper, our librarian, almost went crazy. His favorite subject was a mermaid who was going through a most revealing muscular activity occasioned by a lobster which was just about to nip her where no lady would like it, and the whole thing was mounted on a board in such a way that you could never be sure if the lobster was going to get her, or if she was going to get away. He had fifteen or twenty of these in the exhibit in the library, and Miss Harper told a lot of people she didn't like them. But a good many people who hadn't been in the library in years went in to see the mermaids, and Roger got a lot of encouragement. Shortly after that he put up a sign by his house in the Hollow, advertising an exhibition of woodcarvings at 10¢ admission. I was to see that creep up to a quarter, and finally to 75¢ as the summer trade prostituted our native arts.

A little later he added the word "Hermit" to his name, and Roger was off on a career. He began to add "curios" to his carvings. Nobody knew where he got them, but no doubt he made most of them. He had death masks of a lot of famous people. He had pickled snakes in jars, but folks in town said he whittled them. We thought it was far more interesting to think he had carved out a coiled snake than it was to believe he had imported a real pickled cobra, but the tourist trade wasn't so thoughtful. Amongst some petrified pieces from the "Pee-trified Forest" he had a big white ball, which was probably plaster of Paris, but it sat there unobtrusively unless somebody asked him about it, when he would explain that it was a petrified snowball. A good many people believed it was.

Then he started the rumor that he was 105 years old. He had papers to prove it, even if our town had a number of middle-aged people in it who had gone to school with him, or before him. He grew a beard, and stated the remarkable water from his well had life-giving qualities, and contained the magic ingredient. In the summer, when his well went dry, he would bring in water from other wells and sell it just the same, and a lot of people bought a drink just to see what his magic water tasted like. He had a skull of an Indian he scalped when he was a young man, which showed the grain of good white cedar if you looked closely, but hardly anybody did. He had a drum from Africa with human skin for the head, but he told me about that once. He bought a piece of sheepskin and made the drum, and stained it with coffee to look like the remnant of some poor Congo native. He had the skeleton of a Pygmy in a little box, all in pieces, but it was made of yellow birch, and since Roger didn't know much about human anatomy, he had done some original creating, and my father said some of the Pygmy bones looked like sheep ribs.

For a hermit, he spent less time alone than anybody I ever heard of. All summer long his place was crowded, and he had tickets printed up which he sold you as you came in the front door. People in town didn't have to pay, we were supposed to be in on the deal, and if we happened to be around when anybody came to see the hermit, we were supposed to play some part in the drama. So it happened that some of the curios had a different description every time anybody came, and some of us boys got very proficient in entertaining the customers. I had a rather lengthy speech I used to make about his left-handed tools. A left-handed monkey-wrench has been a joke for a long time, but Hermit Roger discovered once that a good many tools need to be adjusted somewhat for use by a left-handed person. He carried on a one-man crusade to get tool makers to make these changes, and was credited with having persuaded a scissors maker to make left-handed scissors, tin snips, sheep shears, pruning shears, and all such as that. This was all right, and he had all sorts of planes and groovers he'd made to go with them so he could have a display of left-handed tools. But some tools are just the same left as right, so he ran some of these right into the exhibition and was able to piece out quite a display. People who picked up a pair of tin snips and saw they were made to fit a left hand would see the sense in the idea, but a left-handed chisel or a left-handed nail set caused them to look curiously at it to see how it might differ from any nail set. Of course it didn't, and the trick was to keep talking so they would get more and more confused. Roger had also taken advantage of the left-handed thread on a bolt, and had a few things in the exhibition that indicated maybe these were special for left-handed people. It was surprising how many of the summer people showed great interest in a left-hand thread, and thought it was something the hermit had invented. We boys all knew that the left-side wheels on a buggy or wagon had to be put on with a left-hand nut, or they'd come off when you started to drive ahead. If you backed an old-fashioned wagon too far the wheels would come off. So there wasn't too much in the hermit's collection that struck us as wonderful, but he was able to cash in because his customers were uneducated in those things.

There was a belief in town that Roger wasn't very bright, and I suppose he wasn't, but he is the only man I ever heard of who made a living by being a hermit. After a few years he made a practice of going South winters. He made a great to-do over it, and took a lot of his curios with him. In later years he had a big Reo automobile with a trailer behind it, and his going away would sometimes be delayed several times until he felt the town had taken full notice of it. A certain number of people were required to say goodbye, after which he went off in a cloud of dust just when the most of us were getting banking put around the houses. In the spring he would come rushing back, usually with a good many new curios, and everybody was supposed to hurry out and see them and hear about all the splendid things that happened to him down south. It developed in later years that he never got any further south than Connecticut, where he would rent a vacant store and spend the winter displaying his odds and ends, but to our hermit Connecticut was as south as anything could be, and he was never one to carp on strict definitions.

After the business built up the hermit hired an assistant. In later years I have wondered how the government tax experts would react if they saw a taxpayer fill in his occupation as "Assistant To A Hermit." But it was a good job, and paid well. Melvin Warren was the assistant, and had to be at work at seven o'clock in the morning.

So the business went, and the hermit and his assistant gave us much to laugh at, but there was a lot to Roger, and I'm afraid our generation underestimated him. He was probably one of the first people in Maine to realize that these tourists coming up here were willing to be entertained with something besides food and fishing and scenery, which is something a lot of our people haven't found out yet. He left an estate of about thirty thousand dollars, and willed his house and curios to Mel Warren, but Mel didn't have the fire in his head and he didn't succeed. Somehow, with Roger gone, the hermitage wasn't the same, no matter how many people crowded in. So the thing passed away, but it was building up and going strong all the years I was growing up, and there was a good deal to be known about people that I'd never have learned without watching the visitors at Roger's. My mother said that when God made mistakes, He was as likely to lean one way as another, and I think Roger was a genius that didn't get cooked quite enough.

We had others that didn't get cooked even that much, and it is true that the "foolish fellow" was part of our town always. In one respect they were an economic security, because you could hire one of them to do the things you didn't want to do, as cleaning out privies, mowing swalegrass, painting out the gable, or anything such as that. All these foolish fellows had ability if it was directed the right way. We also had feeble-minded people and outright insanity, but that was different. They got put away. But our foolish fellows had a certain ability to keep remotely in touch with events, and were a lot like Neddie Carter, who would take any amount of criticism by saying, "I'm a foolish fellow, and I ain't supposed to know much. Well, by God, I don't, see?" And he was just about right. Neddie was available, though, for odd jobs, and while he was technically a town charge, he never cost the taxpayers a cent, and for every dime he earned he outworked the bright people. It almost seems to me, as I survey the rural scene today, that the foolish fellow has largely disappeared, and I think the reason is that our social betterment programs have elevated him. Modern labor customs include him under the minimum wage law, and he is subject to unemployment compensation and social security along with anybody else. He may have gained stature, but he has lost charm, and society is the loser—because a foolish fellow added to community life and was also a teacher of growing men.

Nobody knew about psychoses and mental blocks in those days, and the foolish fellow wasn't cataloged. Usually somebody was saying of him, "He ain't so foolish as you think—why, one time I saw him," etc. I suppose he was a kind of by-product of breeding, not so much a "case" as he was a planned part of the Almighty's program for mankind. "You can tell what a foolish fellow will do, but watch a crook," is an adage amongst us. We had a family of foolish boys in town, four of them, and we also had another family of eighteen children who were all bright as dollars. One of those in the big family was kidding once, and said, "I suppose that quartet of boys includes the four biggest fools that ever got born." The father of the quartet heard about it and said, "Well, they's only four of them." My father hired one of these foolish boys once to help my mother build a rock garden, at about the time rock gardens were beginning to attract attention. My father happened to walk around the corner of the house during this work, and saw the foolish fellow leaning on a shovel while my mother was boosting on a rock as big as a cow, and the foolish fellow was saying, "Be careful Mrs. Gould, or you'll rupture yourself." My father fired him on the spot, and I had the great honor of being elected to "fill his position," which I did until we got a rock garden of sorts put together. If you want to send my mother off into a gale of laughter now, you just warn her to be careful.

This same fellow was cleaning out a toilet once for Hap Ridlon, the agent of the factory, and Hap pointed to his feet sticking out from under the shed and said to Mrs. Stevens, "I'm dictating to my secretary." That was all this fellow needed, and he had some neat little business cards printed that said, "Secretary Noble, Toilet Expert." The word secretary stuck, and we never called him anything else. Once he heard that the Ladies' Aid of the church was going to put on its annual chicken pie supper, and he came to my mother, who was chairman of the committee, and said he'd like to donate the chickens. He did, and they had a fine supper, and the next day Ken Mason had Secretary arrested for robbing his henhouse. My mother always used to say, "Anyway, he's clean." We always fed the odd jobs men at noon when they were working at our place, and Mother observed that Secretary Noble always washed up very well, slobbering in the sink and blowing until his face shone like a bottle. Some of the bright people who came to work didn't smell too well at table, and Mother was inclined to rate cleanliness above brains.

We had a foolish fellow who claimed he shaved with a blowtorch. He would smear gasoline on his face, he said, and then shave.. Nobody believed him, but one night he entertained the Grange by showing how he did it. He cleaned his whiskers off and left his face all pinky, and also set fire to the Grange Hall. There wasn't much damage, but we could see that a blowtorch would take off whiskers.

We had one fellow who couldn't tell Sunday from a keg of nails, but he was the handiest thing with woodworking tools this world has ever seen. I've seen him stand a board on edge, and bore a five-eighths bit through it edgewise and come out even on the lower side. You couldn't do it, and neither can I. He could saw a board off square without marking it, too. But you couldn't get him to do any cabinet work—all he wanted to do was make birdhouses. He had eight and ten to a tree all around his house, and everybody in town who had a place to hang a birdhouse had bought some from him. And a fellow who came with an empty basket and peddled. He would bring this basket and make believe spread goods out on the steps or on the table, and you were supposed to haggle with him. He'd haggle back, and strike a hard bargain, and then you'd buy some little imaginary thing for a dime or so, and he'd put everything else back in his basket and go off. He got a lot of money that way. We had a foolish fellow who could take care of bees. He liked bees and bees liked him. He used to prove that he could talk to bees by telling a bee to go sting somebody. The bee would then go and sting somebody. The person involved wasn't always pleased, but the rest of us observed that the foolish fellow could talk to bees and they would understand him. One fellow collected swill around town, and the selectmen would buy him baby pigs spring and fall and then buy them back when they were grown. He was so bad he couldn't even talk straight, but he was punctual about his collections, and he learned once to tip his hat to the women. He would come running across the street and tip his hat, and then go back again. Women in town would say, "Thank you, Willie," and Willie was delighted. But swill got collected, and whatever reason God had for making Willie, he served a useful purpose. I understand in some places garbage disposal is a problem, and it may just be that society isn't quite so well off now that everybody is bright.

CAPPY Push-button Palmer was better for me than a post graduate course at Harvard, because I didn't have to leave town to matriculate and it didn't cost me a cent. He was Harbor Master, and in this position he demonstrated how self-sufficient is a Maine town, and how right it was to be free of outside authority. Of course, the state and federal governments have encroached since that time, but I guess a Harbor Master could still surprise you today if you tried to exceed your lawful rights.

The Harbor Master is nothing but a "minor town officer." He gets appointed every April First along with the Fence Viewers, Hog Reeves, Public Weighers, and Inspectors of Hoops, Casks and Shook. Most of these officers have long outlasted any public usefulness, and if they are still appointed it is a tribute to their quondam importance. A few such minor officers still function, more are appointed without functioning. All coastal towns have a Harbor Master, but there is little for him to do today beyond receiving reports of a lost dory, painted green, or hearing a complaint from summer people that a dead seal is casting a disagreeable effluvia upon the beach. Dead seals will do that without half trying, and Cappy wasn't too sympathetic when the complaint came to him. He used to tell them they wouldn't notice it so bad come colder weather. Then they would report to the Selectmen, and the Selectmen would have Honey-Boy Broderick go down and bury the seal. There has always existed in Maine a division of opinion as to who owns a dead seal, and my observation has been that anybody can have it who wants it without stirring up any great amount of dispute. It was a great indignity to suggest that the Harbor Master should have jurisdiction over such, but the summer people didn't appreciate these finer distinctions. The Harbor Master, in short, was class. His former importance in the golden days of sail had been forgotten, and summer people assumed that he must be for something, without realizing that to a great extent that something was as dead as their seals. It was good to have a few such symbols still in action, because it showed us how much we owed to the past. But twice, at least, Cappy Palmer's duties as Harbor Master had rebirth, and I was able to see that our little town had a sovereignty that might be dormant, but which was just as real as it ever was.

Cappy was a hunchback and stood a hair higher than the thwart in a double-ender if he stood on his tiptoes. He had a head that was probably normal for a grown man, but it seemed prodigious on him. Like the Homeric minstrel whose eyesight was the price of the gift of sweet song, Cappy was hunchbacked, but he had a soothing voice and an infinite capacity for yarning. His disfigured body was something we folks never noticed or thought about. I've wondered if, childishly, we boys weren't attracted to him because he was our size. Anyway, he had engaged in numberless heroic encounters, and always came through a hundred percent. He had been a master mariner and had long since retired. Watching him answered any questions about how he made out at sea, because his size and deformity were no handicaps at all. His home was a small shanty on his wharf, and he ran a marine railway and repair shop to give him something to do. The distance to the store was the same by road or wave, but Cappy always rowed his skiff up for groceries.

I think the first time the sovereignty of our little civil division was brought home to me was the night the yacht clubs came into our harbor. I was in Cappy's wharf-home that evening, hearing one of his stories, when a tap came at his door. He opened it and looked up at a man in a gorgeous uniform who saluted as if he were addressing Frobisher, Drake and Hawkins all at once, and said, "I'm looking for the Harbor Master."

"I'm Harbor Master," said Cappy, "At your service, sir."

We were used to these formalities in our town, the old sea captains had the same respect for others that they demanded themselves, and it was customary to keep up the traditions. The man in uniform said, "I'm commodore of the combined Boston, Salem, Marblehead, New Bedford, and so on and so forth yacht clubs," or something like that, "and we want you to assign moorings."

I remember exactly what Cappy said. He said, "You be, be you; you do, do you?" He was very much taken aback. Nothing like that had ever happened before. We looked out, and our little harbor, punkin colored in the rising moon, was alight with lamps, and there were undoubtedly hundreds of small craft there. Cappy scratched his big head with his long fingers, and said, "Why—go ahead, moor where you please. Make yourselves to home. Any place you like."

The commodore smiled and said, "Oh, no—this is your harbor, we want you to assign moorings."

Afterward Cappy explained it to me. It was a question of responsibility. Nothing might happen, but at the same time something might. If the Harbor Master indicated anchorages, things would be on his shoulders. If the yachts just dropped killicks helter-skelter, there might be difficulties. Cappy knew that all the time, but he tried again.

"Ain't no scurry through here, just a few crab-catchers call themselves lobster fishers, and they don't go out nowadays til high noon, and they ain't a thing could snag, foul, crosshaul or give way. Why'n't you just let go, and it'll be all right, glad to have you with us."

But the upshot was that Cappy dragged his double-ender down over the beach and spent the whole night assigning spots on his chart, and patrolling to see that everybody slept well. I went home, and the next morning the whole town turned out to see the yachts. There weren't as many the next morning as there seemed to be in the dark the night before, but it was a whole harbor full of them all the same, and they were a lovely sight. They had miscalculated somehow in their summer cruise up the Gulf of Maine, and came into our harbor to let some slowpokes catch up. We boys paired off two to a punt, and spent the whole forenoon visiting among them, and we decided yachting was something we didn't care much for. Everybody seemed to think he was very well off because he had a boat, and we youngsters were unimpressed by boats as such.

But the commodore came back to Cappy's just before the yachts put out again, and paid him. Cappy said, "Oh, that's all right, glad to have been of service—forget it.

§✺ 64

Come again, come often. Glad to have you with us." But the commodore insisted. He said something about a lawful fee. Cappy said he didn't know what it was. "Don't make no damn's odds what it be, don't want it. Glad to have you with us." So the commodore gave Cappy $100 and said he'd find out what the lawful fee was per boat, and he'd mail the rest. "With something for yourself, of course," he said. He and Cappy saluted as if they were trying to see who'd be last man, and then the yachts went out. Cappy said, "I got a hundred and seventy-five more coming, but I was afraid if I told him the fee he'd say I was graspin'."

But the thing brought home to me the real importance of our Harbor Master. Say what you like, it was Cappy's harbor. He was the boss. And three million dollars' worth of good Massachusetts yachts had just come all the way up to acknowledge it. Cappy knew it, but the custom had so nearly passed that much of the snap had gone from the official routine. I imagine a generation earlier Cappy would have been ordering folks around a good deal, and they'd have acted smart or he'd have seen to it.

It was a summer or two later that Cappy performed as Harbor Master again, and I was around. A United States Navy craft came in and tied up at the old fish-house wharf, on the far side of the harbor. She was a queer looking thing, and the story went around that she was a new type, being tried out at sea, and something had gone wrong. In the afternoon a big government automobile came with a lot of men, and they went aboard, and curiosity ran high. Cappy sat on his wharf and watched, and finally he decided to find out.

Now a phrase runs with the sea around here, and it is, "Got your equipment?" It is the standard salute of the Coast Guard, and when they overhaul you for inspection they ask it. It has become another by-word amongst us, and if you go to my town and ask a random citizen, "Got your equipment?" he might respond, "All secure and ready." There was a time when this exchange concluded the conversation, which was curious because as far as I know nobody ever had his equipment, and there were frequent arguments as to what the equipment was supposed to be, anyway. It was, as nearly as I ever found out, a compass, foghorn, life preservers for everybody aboard, extinguisher, and "two copies of the pilot rules." It included, probably, any registration papers that were required. The two copies of the pilot rules were supplied by the customs office, and were printed in very fine type besides being worded so nobody could understand them anyway. The older folks taught us a simple rhyme that included all essential navigation rules—the old "green to green and red to red" doggerel—and it was much more sensible to have that in your head than it was to have two printed folders in your locker. The compass was another item of dubious value. Everybody had one, but it was always out of whack, and our small boats sailed by ear anyway. Most of them claim to be compass-wise, but I gather that few of our fishermen could sail by compass anyway, even if it was easier. I think if one of them did, he wouldn't admit it. So this query, "Got your equipment?" ran through out coastal customs, and it had an official ring that demanded the courtesy of a proper reply. I imagine if our old Coast Guard had found an enemy fleet sailing into New York Harbor they'd have begun negotiations by asking, "Got your equipment?" The thing was that well established.

So Cappy got in his punt and rowed over to the old fish-house wharf, and to the sailor working on the deck of the queer vessel he called, "Got your equipment?"

The sailor leaned over the rail, surveyed the punt

with its pint-sized occupant, and said, "What in Hell are you?"

Cappy was unoffended. He might have preferred "who," but that was unimportant. Cappy held respect for the Navy, and was not to be teased into discourtesy. Cappy shipped one oar and pulled the pins, and said, "I'm Harbor Master!"

Then the seaman did a curious thing. He stepped back to attention, snapped out a salute, and said, "One moment, sir, I'll report below." He stuck his head into a hatch, and then backed away and straightened up. Out of the hatch came three Navy officers in full uniform, one of them with a fore-and-aft hat all wiped and plumed, and they lined up and saluted Cappy with every evidence of respect. Cappy was flustered, and said so afterward, and all he could do was repeat, "Have you got your equipment?" A little smile came to the Navy, then, and they asked him to step aboard and he did so while the seaman caught the line from his punt.

Well, Cappy had a grand time. They treated him fine. They told him the whole story of the vessel, and showed him the engines, and insisted on getting out their papers while Cappy insisted he didn't want to put them to no trouble. Everything was in order, as far as Cappy could tell, and he said it was a magnificent craft and must have cost a cool fortune. He said they had a wireless that spit fire, and that was quite a piece of equipment in those days. Cappy stayed to supper with them, and showed the cook how to get a little better action out of his cream-tartar biscuits, and about dark they brought him back across the harbor in a power launch, towing his double-ender astern, all standing on one end.

So we saw that the Harbor Master was to be reckoned with, even by the Navy, and naturally that is right. It was our harbor, Cappy's, and we had a town's bounden right to know what went on in it. In time of war, maybe we could ease up a bit, but that was to be seen. Ours was the only harbor in the world that mattered to us, then, and it was all ours. Cappy had the town behind him, and not even an admiral in an admiral's hat had any more. Cappy was forever telling, after that, how an admiral saluted him once. "He bowed quite a good deal whilst he done it, too," Cappy would say. And he should have. As Harbor Master, Cappy was a dignitary, too.

"Tell me a story, Cappy," I'd say when I wandered into his front room where the geraniums in tin cans outlined the forefront of his harbor view. Away out beyond the sheltering islands and the points, on a bright day, the white hairline of Bullhorse Rock Light cut the horizon. At night the light practically pounded the windowpanes—three seconds yellow, two seconds dark, and then one second red. He would sit there with his own light off and watch it hour upon hour until bedtime. In a southerly, when the fog obliterated the world and night left his front window a gaping black void, the heavy roar of Bullhorse would vibrate the whole front of his home—a thundering, joyless sound that was its own kind of coastal music. Cappy liked it. Cappy told the story of the man who blew the whistle every ten seconds for three weeks one August, and then when the mechanism failed and the whistle skipped a toot, the man jumped up and said, "What was that?" I heard the story within the year on a radio program, and it was probably funny to a lot of people. It wasn't to me— I was suddenly back in Cappy's little front room, which isn't there any more, and neither is Cappy.

Once a little yawl came into our harbor, and Cappy went out to see if he could find out who it was, and if he could make them feel at home. They were honeymooners, yachting along the coast. Cappy pointed out the store to them, and they went ashore for groceries. Then Cappy

climbed to their masthead and tied a codline. He took
the other end of the codline ashore and tied it to his
doorknob. After the honeymooners had supper and put
out their lamps, Cappy began to saw on the codline, and
in no time he had the little yawl rocking like a teeter
board. A line like that to the topmast can give a terrific
purchase. Cappy could have rocked the Queen Mary with
one finger, that way. He sawed all night and the next
morning before daybreak he eased off, and went out and
cut the codline and came ashore and went to bed. The
honeymooners told everybody what a rough night it had
been, and folks around the store were grieved to think
our snug little harbor, that was like a millpond even in a
no'theaster, could act up so. The honeymooners said it
was pretty bad.

One time Cappy was chipping ice off his railway and
he fell overboard. Maybe I should explain that a marine
railway is just an incline on which boats are taken from
the water into storage, or into a repair shed. If ice forms
too heavily on one in the winter, the tide will lift the
water-end and cause damage. Cappy would push his punt
out and stand up in it and chop at the ice every few days
at low water slack. So he fell overboard, and found the
water was as cold as usual in the winter, and thought it
would be a good idea to get out of it. He swam for the
ladder on his wharf, but just as he was about to put a hand
on it, a rope of some sort under water snagged him up
short. He didn't know what the rope was, couldn't imagine how it got there, and it puzzled him. He swam out
to a spile and clung to it for a minute, trying to dislodge
his rope. He thought he had it off, so he swam for the
ladder again, but he got snagged up again. This kept up
for quite a number of times, and as the tide was coming
all the time the spile began to be too far under water to
be of much help. At last he had to stand on the top of it

when he got to it, and then his chin was just awash. Each time he was about to reach the ladder, the rope brought him up short, and he told me the only thing that kept him going was his recollection of his mother.

"Mother used to say, 'Dennis, you'll never drown. You'll never drown. You'll hang. You'll hang as high as Haman.' So I kept trying, because I didn't want to disappoint my poor old mother." The rope finally "gave" a little, and Cappy was able to get both hands on a rung of the ladder. There he stayed—exhausted. The rope held his feet out taut, and his hands clung outstretched to the ladder. Then the tide went out. "And left me hanging higher than Haman and then some," said Cappy. He hung there until somebody found him, and they carried him a clinking jingle of ice into his front room and cracked him like a walnut to get his clothes off. They tried to get him to take some whiskey, but he said he didn't want to die with a brown taste in his mouth, and he'd rather wait until he could enjoy it. The men said they could hear his teeth chattering out on the wharf and away up on the street, but Cappy snapped out of it in no time, and was back on the next afternoon tide chipping ice again. Cappy was always coming through such things while robust, normal men died a thousand deaths.

His own boat was the Dolphin, and she had a Diesel engine that would send her around 20 knots. She was easily the fastest boat anywhere around, but Cappy rarely opened her up. He never fished in her, and seldom took anybody with him. He liked to cruise, and every summer would load her up and be gone for two or three weeks. One summer he was jogging along and fell in with an Arctic expedition. They went right on up inside the Arctic Circle, and Cappy with them, as pleased as could be and having an awful good time. It began to get embarrassing. The explorers wanted to put in somewhere and get some sleep and play cribbage, and think up their lectures for the next season, and here was Cappy gumming up the whole program. He caught on after a while and turned about and came home. He brought a lot of things, including a narwhale horn about six feet long. He used to say the other one got broken off, or he'd have had the head mounted. He gave me a walrus tusk, and I still have it.

One of Cappy's many innovations with marine machinery was his air whistle. Cappy had a certain ability that way, and earned his title of "Push-button Cappy" honestly. In those days the small boats carried a tin horn to blow if it fogged, and if a man took his fog seriously he'd blow his head off coming up through the islands. So Cappy devised a compressor that worked on his engine, and set up an air tank with a whistle on it. It sounded a lot like one of our modern Diesel locomotive whistles, and everybody wanted one but Cappy intended to keep it for himself as long as there was novelty to it.

Well, one night he was on his way out from Portland, and it was a pretty night and he swung inside the islands and watched the scenery. It was pleasant jogging along, seeing the lights in the farms and cottages along the shore, and Cappy was entranced by the peace and loveliness of the times. He lit up his pipe. And as he cupped his hands around the flame of the match, sea-fashion, and turned into the wind, he had his face right up against the air gauge on his whistle tank. He saw what the gauge said out of the corner of his eye, and there was a split second when it didn't register with him. But only a split second, because the gauge said 387 pounds.

What Cappy did was a marvel of quick-thinking and pussy-cat dexterity. He realized his safety valve had failed to blow, and the impounded air had only one outlet—through the whistle. So he grabbed the whistle cord, opened a hatch, thrust the cord through, and closed the hatch on it so the whistle would be kept blowing. Then he threw the wheel over hard so the Dolphin would circle and jammed his bilge pump over against it to hold the position. Then he jumped overboard.

If that air tank had blown up, not one particle of Cappy and his Dolphin would have been found. A blast like that would sink a battleship. Cappy climbed into his punt when it went by—he was towing it on two or three fathoms of line, and as he couldn't think of anything else to do at the moment, he sat there while the Dolphin slowly circled in the night and her whistle poured forth an ear-splitting blast that knew neither beginning nor end. The engine kept pumping more air, so the whistle kept blowing more noise, and Cappy kept sitting there because there was nowhere else to go. People on the islands and points came out to look into the night and wonder what it was, and some of them came out in their boats to inquire. Cappy tried yelling at them, first, but the whistle made that useless, so afterward he just sat there with his arms folded and rode and rode around and around.

Then somebody called the Coast Guard, and the Coast Guard came and lit the thing up with searchlights until Cappy stood up in his punt and cursed at them and shook his fist. Every time he came around they would ask him if there was anything they could do, and Cappy would tell them to go to Hell, but the whistle prevented a clear exchange of ideas, and nobody did anything except Cappy, and he just sat there and rode. By this time the shore line was crowded with interested spectators, and speculation was rife as to what was going on, and almost everybody for miles and miles up and down the long bay was curious. Along towards morning the fuel ran out in the Dolphin. Then Cappy went aboard and unscrewed the whistle and borrowed some Coast Guard oil to get home on, and it was a number of weeks before he could hear a word that anybody said to him. He made a few changes in his whistle mechanism after that, with a view to greater safety in the future, but most of the time he ran about with the compressor disconnected, and he would gladly have sold whistles to other boats if they had cared for one.

So Cappy spun his yarns for me, and I grew up. And one day as he sat thinking about a good many unrelated incidents, he got a bright idea, and he rowed up to the Town Landing and went to the office of the Selectmen and made them a proposition. He told them he'd deed all his property to the Town if the Town would care for him at the Poor Farm as long as he lived. The arrangement, as proposed, was highly illegal in those days, as Towns were limited in their functions to the bare duties of government, and a contract like that was outside the possibilities. But they took him on, and he was delighted. He had no family at all. So he moved one day up to the Town Farm, and was there 17 years before he was done with his life. He never set eye on salt water again, but for 17 years he remained the duly appointed Harbor Master. He had his little room to himself, three meals a day, some spending money, his tobacco and his whiskey. He had thoughtfully bargained for writing paper, and a few small items like that. He was as happy as could be, and was grateful to the Town for accepting his proposal.

I went in to see him just a few months before he died. The Town had wanted to sell the Poor Farm for years, because the newer ideas of social betterment were becoming popular, and certain do-gooders had evolved the notion that a Poor Farm was a disgrace. Cappy might have confused them a little, because he was perfectly happy, and liked the idea first rate. The Town sold the farm a couple of months after Cappy went, but as long as he lived they were stuck with it. He tried to tell me another story, that day, but he couldn't control his words. A doctor told me what ailed him—it was a long word I had no trouble forgetting promptly. He couldn't say the word he wanted, but said all those that rhymed with it. If the word was "fine," he would say dine, mine, sign, pine and so on until he either hit the right one, or saw that I comprehended. In the end we sat there smoking together and saying nothing. He was a great old Cappy.

His last bargain with the town was fulfilled. The granite marker on his cemetery lot was part of the arrangements. It has a pretty good view of our little harbor, which was Cappy's Harbor all the time I was growing up, and it says on it exactly what he stipulated: Capt. Dennis J. Palmer, Harbor Master.

Saunders

IN MAY we hung Maybaskets, and I gather the custom is mostly State of Maine. I don't know why this is so, because Maybaskets made a magnificent excuse to get out in the springtide and be joyful. The politics of May Day passed us by. May was meant for Maybaskets, and we hung them all month long in a sweaty helter-skelter of running and hiding that unfolded to us more or less a great many wonderful things. Nobody seems to know where the idea started, but a Maybasket was a gaudy, crepe-paper gift that you brought to your best true love in the warmth and promise of a May twilight. As May wore along, you found you had a number of best true loves, no two alike and all different, and after about three weeks the thing degenerated until you were hanging Maybaskets to almost anybody.

Mother wasn't too far removed from the gay doings herself—I was the oldest in the family—so she helped me get my first Maybasket ready. It was a shoe box all primped and festooned with gay colors and paper flowers, with braided loops for handles. It looked rich, and it held some gingersnaps and filled cookies, an orange and a lollypop, a handful of nuts and some fudge. It was the finest thing I have ever seen, and it certainly would please Grace. Grace was a lovely blonde who lived through the woods and beyond a pasture, and was just the young lady for such a fine Maybasket. Mother said she ought to be pleased.

The lilacs were on the way, and the whole countryside was alive again after the mean things our April did to spring. The stars were beginning to come out. May is designed for Maybaskets, because the sun doesn't take all afternoon to go down, and darkness comes with the doing of the supper dishes. A boy can hang a Maybasket to his girl after dark, and still not stay up past bedtime. So I struck out. I had to hold the box up high so it wouldn't drag on the ground, and the trip through the woods was slow. The fences bothered. Over the second one I could see the light in her kitchen window.

Of course she'd be home. No proper young lady, in Maine, is away from home on the first of May. It just isn't done. I looped the handles of the Maybasket over the front doorknob and tolled the bell. It was one of those bells with a pull-wire. The wire runs all around inside the house and eventually dings the bell. I had no way of knowing the wire was broken, so I pulled it periodically for the next half hour or so and ran each time to hide behind the syringa bush. Then I took the Maybasket around to the back door like a human being, and knocked. I was hardly in the lee of the apple tree when the door opened and Grace's father poked his head out. He didn't see it at first, because it had dropped off the knob with a most unromantic plop, and lay in a heap on the steps. Then he saw it, and turned into the house with, "Gracie! Maybarskit!"

Life brings many pleasures, but life has nothing to offer like the shriek of a youthful blonde who has received her first Maybasket. It was such a shriek as proved beyond all logic that Gracie was delighted. She picked up the Maybasket and went into the kitchen and shut the door. Now this is the critical period, and is part of the routine. If a girl picks up the basket and goes in the house, and doesn't come out again all evening, you have the right to assume that she is unworthy of your ardent suit. You might as well go home. But if, through the window, you can see her stoop down to pull on her rubbers, and all the time she is running about the kitchen as if she has bees in her hair, you are safe to assume that she is on your side. You can expect that shortly she will burst out into the night wild-eyed and eager, and that the spice and ginger of an early romance will be upon you.

Gracie did just that. She jumped off the top step and landed ten feet out in the dooryard running like a deer, splitting the night air with whoops of delight. We were alone at last in the rich warmth of a May evening. How old were we? That's hard to say. May is such a fine time, and the springtime of a Maine youth imparts special wisdom. In Maine you sometimes grow up fast. It doesn't take long to do it. I think it's the iodine in the air, but they tell me that is absurd. Gracie called me and ran all around and called me again, and then she found me behind the tree and squealed. The chase was on!

Now this particular chase, being my first, is one I remember in great detail. The first great discovery that came to me, as I sped around the house, was the location of the clothesline. I found it when it sang under my chin. Momentum set in at that moment, and although I made my feet go with great energy, this exercise had nothing whatever to do with my progress. The line sang taut, and my neck played upon it with gusto, and then the thing shot me out of the bow, sort of, and I landed on Gracie who was following up her advantage of knowing that particular dooryard better than I did. Gracie was speechless for a few moments, but upon recovery she lit out again, and we went around the house the other way. My next discovery was the location of Mr. Mercer's cultivator. It was a two-horse cultivator with wings attached, and I found it with one knee in such an intimate fashion that I set it back in the yard about ten feet and stirred up the sodground considerably. While I was pondering this great find, Gracie landed on me with all seventeen feet and made me decide that further flight was useless.

That was the idea—the young lady had to catch her admirer, and then she was to kiss him. The kiss might have made a more lasting impression on my memory if I hadn't just been overwhelmed by the ardent protestations of the cultivator. Gracie fetched her father and mother, and they carried me tenderly into the kitchen while Gracie tagged along in tears and kept saying, "Is it broken? Is it broken?" I felt it was, but I didn't know in how many pieces, but Gracie's father insisted it was just a bruise and I would be all right. He was correct, and by September I could walk again with only the most imperceptible limp. Then we had some raspberry shrub and some lemon cookies, and we sat around the kitchen until it was time for me to go home. Gracie's mother told me it was time for me to go home, so I got up and went home. It was dark in the woods, and the fences sneaked up on me, and my knee hurt to glory, but it had been a wonderful night and Gracie had been perfect. She moved away a year or so afterward, and I have often wondered whatever became of her. Each time I have so wondered a peculiar twinge has come to my left knee, and I doubt if I ever forget my first Maybasket.

I'd have hung her more Maybaskets if she'd stayed

around, I know it. Cultivator and all, I'd have hung many of them. Cultivators were nothing, we found them everywhere. Maybasket time is a time to race at top speed through the dark, and anything in the way must simply look out. A Jersey cow makes a nice thing to run into, particularly one that is lying down and has to stand up when you bump her to make sure she doesn't miss anything. A cow on which you are laid out stunned would do much better to remain seated. A greenhouse is also a good find, but the best thing of all is a well. An open well will sometimes catch several boys in one evening, and a mystery of well-construction is how they ever stoned them up so a boy doesn't brain himself in the descent. A boy can pitch into a fifteen-foot well, all arms and legs, and nothing happens to him except he gets wet. A well really isn't very cold, it only seems cold because you have been running. There is always a stone you can hang to, or a pump pipe you can shin up.

If you have to stay there until found, you discover that the science of acoustics in wells has had extremely little attention. There is much to be done in that field. Some means should be found to disperse the noise and make it available to people up above. When the boy pops to the top of the water and yells so his tongue tries to get out of the way, at first he has the impression that a bull has blatted in his ear. He looks all around in the dim light, and discovers he did it himself. The yelp echoes back and forth in the well for quite some time, thumping you as it goes by, and you decide it will be much better to maintain a merciful silence. The fact is that a person up on the ground, three feet back from the well, couldn't hear you with an ear trumpet no matter how good his ears are, and all the noise you are making goes straight up in the air and never comes back. If somebody chances to miss you, and wonders to himself, "I wonder, now, if he's in the well," and goes over to look down, you can part his hair with the slightest whisper. You do not, however, whisper. You let him have it. And in a moment he has let down a rope and you are back running around as if nothing had happened. On all well-regulated Maybasket parties, somebody will look down the well every so often.

These parties were different from the individual hangings that were coupled blithely with romance. We went in groups to hang Maybaskets, too. Everybody would chip in a dime or a nickel, and a committee would buy a box of chocolates. If the box cost a dollar and the kitty stopped at 95¢, the storekeeper was expected to assist and attend by proxy. This kind of a hanging usually involved the school teacher, or almost anybody if the month was getting along. In late May we were sometimes hard put to find hangees, and almost always went up and hung one to a maiden lady on the sunrise side of Poppycock Hill who was a good chaser. It was a shame that she never had a chance to chase somebody her own age, because I think it would have greatly pleased him, but for some reason it wasn't to be. We all got kissed soundly by this poor woman, and thought it was quite a lark. I believe now that we brought her much pleasure. She'd ask us in after she caught the boys, and we'd play games and have something to eat, and then we'd feel our way back through the heavy trees that covered Poppycock Hill, every boy helping some timid girl along, and sometimes it took quite a good deal of time to effect a safe and successful trip home.

Our teachers probably saw through these parties. They got Maybaskets because we wanted to get out in a crowd in the night and have fun. They must have known that. But we hung them one dutifully, and they usually delegated the catching and removed all that fun. A teacher could always catch the fat, waddly, near-sighted girl with the freckles, and then she'd say, "There—now you catch the rest." After a few minutes we'd walk in and be tagged, and then make use of the balance of the evening otherwise. Teachers always received Maybaskets as if it were in their contracts. All except one. I remember one who was much too young to be trusted with us growing Maine boys, although she pulled through. She was as pretty as the law permits, and in May we hung her a Maybasket. She leapt out onto the lawn and whooped after us, and she caught and kissed every last boy, and we loved her passionately. The day after we hung her the Maybasket she came to school and spoke about it. She said it was wonderful that we did it, and it made her so happy. She said where she grew up, in Massachusetts, they didn't hang Maybaskets, and she wouldn't have known what to do except that Mr. Whitcomb warned her. Mr. Whitcomb was chairman of the school board, and he was thoughtful. He is also dead and gone and his place has been taken by a new breed, and I'll bet no school board since has ever instructed a teacher in how to receive a Maybasket.

I shudder to recall the things that happened those evenings when we Maybasketed. We were uninhibited completely, as pagans should be for their ceremonial rites. We ran wild. We never perpetrated anything beyond the call of duty, and we never got into any trouble that brought bad odor on Maybasketing. We climbed over roofs, and fell over ledges and frolicked unseemly, but we seldom got hurt, and May passed altogether too quickly. The best of it, of course, was to come in years afterward, when May struck again, and we would see the young fry going off in the dusk with their May-paper baskets. Thoughts might shift a thousand different ways, but somehow to me Maybaskets mean, most of all, a particular night when the moon was low and full, and six of us, three boys and three girls alternating, stood on the top of Poppycock Hill hand to hand, and looked out across the ocean to the Azores and beyond, and just stood there and looked, and thought how pretty it was. I remember the six, and I remember them mostly for that. It was the night of all nights, and the Maybasket had been hung to the maiden lady and we were on our way home. Nothing permanent came of it as this world's affairs are measured. It was just a moment, and then we had turned and shifted hands and were coming down the hill on our way home. Our shadows reached out ahead of us in the road, and then we walked on into the darkness under the trees, and hand in hand we knew we were there. But there was no voice, and our feet tread silently on the pine needles.

May was always the shortest of all the months, and then there came a year when May was never to come again. You have to be, really, just that age. And I wouldn't wonder if you have to be, really, in just that place.

Then came June, and we had a thing called a Junebasket. Nobody ever hung one—it was just a thing you joked about. You were supposed to take a box and fill it with stable manure, and leave it on the steps of somebody you didn't like. This was supposed to engender ill will and a nasty feeling, and there was a tendency on the part of the hangee to get mad over it. I never knew of one to be hung, but we used to speak of Junebaskets as if we knew of scarcely anything that was more fun.

ONCE a circus went bankrupt in our town, right across the street from my house, and that is another story. But after the settlement was made, and it came time to move the circus on, a man tried to hire help around town. A lot of the boys and men offered to help put the gear back on the wagons, and among them was Percy Buker, who wasn't very bright.

"And what can you do?" the man asked Percy.

Percy said, "I can saw ice to beat Hell."

This was Percy's total claim to fame, and it goes to show that no matter how mean and temporary a skill is, if a man is proud of it, it will suffice. Percy could saw ice to beat Hell, and that was all he lived for. Two weeks come every January gave him his chance to prove, again, that nobody could outsaw him. The town's ice pond was his arena, and people actually stood around in the sub-zero cold and watched him. It was quite a sight.

I'm not sure it wouldn't be smart to describe how

we cut ice. The day has passed, and the description might have real historical value. Today, if they cut a pond at all, they use a power saw with a gasoline motor, and Percy is out of a job. In Percy's time, and mine, an ice saw was a coarse-toothed tool about the same length as a one-man crosscut, except that the handle-bar handle was on crosswise. Percy straddled the line he was sawing, and bobbed the saw up and down between his feet.

Ice was cut when the cold weather following the January thaw had thickened it to about 14 inches. The ice man kept his eye on the thickness, and when things were just right he sent out his call. Filling the big rambling ice houses was a great concern of the whole town, because the electric refrigerator was yet to be dreamed up, and manufactured ice was a crazy idea. Everybody who could turn out, turned—even to the minister. We got paid according to what we did, right down to those of us boys who did nothing but tow the long ribbons of ice from the head of the pond down to the runway with a hooked pole. Those were the days of horses, and the teams went onto the pond first with a giant scoop to draw off the drifted snow.

Big Horace Fairchild owned the ice business. He had a voice like the trump of doom, and people who despised him the rest of the year would step around when he bossed them on the pond. Horace's horses scooped off the snow, and then men with axes chopped a hole in the ice where the runway would start. This runway was made of timbers and oak strips. A carriage operated with cable and pulleys by a team of horses up on the bank would lift four cakes of ice at a time to the level of the ice house. Once they left this returnable carriage, the cakes would slide with their own weight into the houses where crews would tier them up.

Down on the pond, where the hole had been chopped

through, Percy Buker had already inserted his ice saw, and was bobbing up and down worse than any monkey on any stick as he sawed right off down the pond. There was some cheering when he got into stride—not that anybody was impressed, but because Percy expected it and it puffed him up to greater speed. A grooving machine had already marked the pond off into strips and cross-strips, so every cake that would go in was outlined to a depth of four or five inches. Percy followed the outside groove, then repeated on the next groove, and so cut out a strip of ice one cake wide. There was a trick to this—the strip had to be cut so it flared out at the bottom, because these cakes were pushed down under, given a half twist, and brought up sidewise into the hole. Then sidewise, they were floated out to the runway and the carriage, and the first cakes went up and into the house. It took quite a while for Percy to do this, during which time everybody was waiting and drawing pay, so Percy bobbed and bobbed until an intelligent man would have been crazy. Percy was supposed to be crazy anyway, and was just the man for the job. They always said that God in his infinite wisdom provided for all the needs of mankind, and no doubt He made Percy on purpose so he could saw ice to beat Hell.

Then we all went to work. After Percy sawed the end cakes, we split off the long strips of ice, one by one. The teamsters trotted the two pairs of horses around the circle up on the bank, and the men on the pond tried to keep ahead of them. The teamsters were happy when they could snake the carriage half-way up the runway before ice had been put in it. The men at the runway tried to keep four cakes in position so the carriage would automatically fall over them each time it descended. If the teamsters were extra fast, we boys on the pond dragged our stomachs sore bringing up ice fast enough. There was a good deal of shouting, and a lot of horseplay, and over everything hung the indescribable cold of a January morning on a Maine ice pond. We wondered if the thermometer would get up to zero that day, and being cold at ice cutting was so much a part of the job that we were unhappy when it did. Ten below was about right.

The first time I ever showed up to help with the ice harvest, Big Horace singled me out and said, "Where's your belt?" He sent me up to the toolhouse to get a piece of twine to wrap around my middle, because a belt was the secret of keeping warm on the job. No matter how many clothes you had on, you could stand there in the wind and freeze if you hadn't drawn a big belt tight around your equator. Men who were thin and wiry in the July hay fields would show up for January ice cutting like roly-poly kewpie dolls, a belt drawn at their middles, and when the wind howled they didn't mind a bit. Nobody knows how that wind can howl if he hasn't been there.

Up inside the ice house, though, the men were stripped to the waist and the sweat rolled off them so, as they said, they sealed the cakes together in a solid mass. We had a fellow who looked like Abe Lincoln, although his intellectual capacities were leaner, and he used to stand at the end of the runway and catch the cakes with a hook. He'd give them a sly twist, just so, and their own momentum would serve to flop them into place in the tiers. A cake of ice always weighed at least 200 pounds, and catching a day's supply of them as fast as they could come was not boy's play. But Merton would laugh and shout, and as I think back now I suppose he got something like $21 for a seven-day week, ten or twelve hours a day. And he was satisfied. His only complaint was that an ice house, at 40 below on a windy day, was stuffy, and the teamsters didn't slack off frequently enough so he could take time to drink a little water.

There were certain people who counted on the ice

harvest to pick up a couple of weeks' pay, but anybody who could arrange his other business would help if he could. And amongst these would be found all the half-wits for miles around, because ice was a good chance to employ the "strong backs and weak heads." The foolish fellows were always falling in the pond. Most of us quickly found out that the margin all around would taper off some as the water worked it. Contrary to popular opinion, the ice is not above the water. The water comes right up in the hole after you've taken the ice out, and sometimes if the ice sags water will come right out over the top. This freezes the groovings in again and calls for repeating the grooving. So we learned that the edge was slippery, and we treated it with respect.

It was the practice of Big Horace to ward off pneumonia among the immersed help by pouring each victim a water tumbler of cheap whiskey, which would burn and sear on the way down, and would make a fellow forget all about having a chill. I fell in once, and hadn't gone down half way before I realized the prize wasn't worth competing for. The water is not cold, comparatively speaking. Obviously it isn't down to 32 degrees, so to a certain extent the sensation of cold is an illusion. The under side of an ice pond is a beautiful shade of turquoise that no artist has ever painted. It is a pity that so few people who would appreciate it have ever seen it. It takes quite a while to stop going down and to begin coming up again, and you feel you have been away for such a long time that it will be a lot of fun responding to any greetings that may be communicated to you by the welcoming committee on the bank. A feeling of disgust comes over you when you pop up and find that the men on the bank are not overly grieved at your predicament. There they stand grinning away like devils, and each of them has a hook on a pole that is presently to be inserted around about your clothing.

A pork chop on a platter, about to be assaulted by a hungry family of fifteen, would know how it feels. And then you are on the ice, and trotting up to the toolhouse and the fire, and if you look you will see that the flow of ice into the house hasn't been slowed a bit by your rash recess.

The toolhouse had a stove in it, with wires overhead where the "Baptists" could hang their clothes to steam. Nail kegs were there to sit on, with a Western Story to read, and a cribbage board and cards that weren't much good unless you had a partner. One day somebody drove a team into the pond, and two men with it. They were re-grooving after a freeze-up, and the whole team and groover went in, with the driver, and the other man still holding the handles of the groover. All he had to do was let go of the handles, but he didn't think that fast, and he grooved right off into the water. Another team was trotted down from the cable work on the runway, and they hooked ropes around the heads of the horses in the water and dragged them out. It stretched their necks some, and they squealed a good bit, but out they came, and they had to be trotted around all afternoon until they were dry so they wouldn't get horse-ail. The two men went to the toolhouse to finish up the bottle and dry off.

I forgot they were in there, so in a little while I went up to get one of the men a sharper hook. When I opened the door the two men were sitting stark naked on nail kegs, pegging away at the cribbage board, and the steam from their drying clothes gave everything the appearance of something out of Vergil or Dante. Particularly when they spoke to me sharply about opening the door on their exposed tenderness, and asked if I wanted them to catch a death. The aroma of drying wool, whiskey, and tobacco was a scintillating experience I never expect to forget.

There is one thought comes to mind here, and that concerns the presence of a boy in this more or less man's work. There was always the greatest deference shown us boys, and although we heard cussing of an advanced and highly rhetorical character, for the most part our tender years were regarded as a public responsibility. At noon, when we opened the great dinner baskets, some man would sometimes start off on a ripper, and somebody would say, "Mind the boys are here." And the story would trail off into an innocent and vapid, and usually disappointing, nothingness. The conclusion was not warranted by the opening remarks. In those days "coarse" work was not beneath the dignity of cultured men, and the crowd on the ice pond included everybody in a fellowship of labor that probably is not destined to come again for a long time. Some of the best minds in town were there on the pond with the teamsters and half-wits, and everybody got along. There was much concern among the men that the boys should learn how to do things, that they should master the tricks and shortcuts. And it is a wonderful day when the growing boy discovers that he is being treated by men as an equal. Without condescension or special attention, but as he should be. Boys grew up more quickly then, and men had more of boyhood in them. That day I fell in the ice pond, it was fine to see that I was expected to take my ducking along with the rest, and go up and dry out, and even have the slug of whiskey if I wanted to, and come back when I was ready and go to work. That same ice-cutting I spoke up for the first time around the dinner boards, and got listened to. No matter what the subject was, I said something—and it got listened to, and the conversation went on as if I'd made a contribution, and not an interruption. About that time a boy can begin calling men by their first names. Among Maine men, Mister is a Town Meeting term, and should not be employed to pad out conversation. You come to be a man, in Maine, by what you do and how much you know—not by who you are. So the boys worked along with the men at cutting ice, and I think an ice pond was an educational institution.

Times have changed, of course. Instead of perpetuating its educational institution with public funds, the town gave up cutting ice entirely, and if anybody wants any today he can get it trucked in from an ammonia plant that freezes fish and makes ice on the side. I happen to think that's too bad, but I don't expect the ice pond to flourish again on its merits as a maker of men. The world is too much, today, like that man who was moving the circus. He was so focused on his own petty needs that he couldn't understand what a great achievement it really is to be able to saw ice to beat Hell.

IT WAS easy to see why that circus went bankrupt in the field across from our house, because by the time the tents were up almost every man, woman and child in town had found some way to get in for nothing. The long-delayed walkout of the unpaid performers could be delayed no more, and here we were with a circus all set up in the field we had just finished mowing. And no evident likelihood that it would be taken down for a long time.

No doubt somewhere in the lore of circuses, some tanbark fan has given literature a good account of just what goes on in a bankrupt circus, even as they have long chronicled the forlorn but joyous adventures of the boy who ran away to live with a lion tamer and grow up to do a wire act and marry a bareback rider. Well, we had no desire to run away and join a circus. We had a circus join us, and there it sat in the field with the flags flying and the lion roaring, and it got so after a few days we didn't care too much about circuses anyway.

Ours was never a circus town. We had a Wild West show come one year, and my uncle put it out of business, then we had the circus come the next year and fold up. It was a bad luck town for them. My uncle really did give the Wild West show the works, and had a lot of fun. It was true that a plain wheat rancher from the Great Plains cut less ice in our town of world-wanderers than he might have in a less traveled section. The Wild West show gave him a chance to prove his stories. And our front piazza gave the community a perfect grandstand from which they could survey his triumph without the formality of tickets, because from our front porch you could look right over the sidewalls into the arena.

When the Wild West show came to town one of the men came to our house and asked if he could get water. He wanted a couple of barrels a day for cooking and washing, and he would be there two days. He was all bejangled and spurred, and had a hat on him as big as a dining-room table, and walked as if he was still riding a horse. My uncle looked up and saw this completely unexpected sight, and permitted himself a reversion to good western-story form, and said, "Well, Old Alkali Charlie himself—where you driving?" The man said, "I beg your pardon?" My Uncle said, "I mistook you for a friend of mine that got an eye punched out looking through a keyhole, but I see you have been able to keep your eyesight intact. What part of the West you from, Tucson?"

This was quite a speech for my uncle, who seldom related any of his Western tales except under great pressure, and who tried in a town of sea captains to keep his place. The man from the show admitted he was born and brought up in Tenafly, N. J., and the closest he'd ever been to the West was to buy things mail order from St. Louis. But my uncle went back with him across the street and surveyed the show, and met all the performers, and found a couple of real cattle hands, and had himself a wonderful time. He sat out on the front porch the first afternoon and enjoyed the spectacle immensely. He was much taken with the bucking broncho, which bucked for $500 if you could stay on him once around the track and nobody could. After the show my uncle went across the street and told them it was a fine show and he enjoyed it a lot, and then he saddled up the bucking broncho and rode him all over town. The man who owned the show was mad about it, said it was a dirty trick. He'd spent years training the pony, and he thought my uncle, even if he was a good rider, ought to respect a man in his trade. My uncle said he was sorry, that he didn't mean any harm, he just admired the pony and thought it would be nice to feel a good horse under him again. My uncle said he'd tell him what he'd do—to make up. He'd ride the pony in the arena the next day for $500, and would let him buck, and he'd tell all around town what was going to happen, and they'd get a real crowd out. And he wouldn't take the $500 either.

So the next day everybody came to see my uncle ride the trick pony and win $500, except that they didn't go in through the gate on tickets, they came and sat on our porch, or stood on the lawn, and there weren't above ten or fifteen people on the inside. But that was enough to give the pony his show-ring confidence, and he came up with an awful buck and knocked my uncle into a heap in the corner. Everybody had seen Uncle riding the horse, so they believed the whole thing was a put-up job, and the man who ran the show was satisfied my uncle had acted nobly. The only trouble was the size of our front porch as contrasted with the income at the box office, and the show departed our town in a ruined state. My uncle thought the whole thing had been a great deal of fun.

But a Wild West show that features your own uncle

was nothing compared with a circus that you could go in and out of at any time of the day, with a real wild man all the wilder because he didn't have the price of a ticket home to Fredericton, N.B. It's too bad boys and girls today don't have a chance to see that kind of a circus. Its greatest attribute was its complete optimism about the chances of entertaining people. It was a one-ring circus, a one-lunger. It had a most lovely lion, who roared constantly. It had an elephant, a real elephant who was very old and inured. An inured elephant was best for our circuit. The camel and giraffe, also, were inured. They had about 35 trained dogs to complete the menagerie, which was quite a bundle of dogs when you were trying to set up a tent amongst them. Somebody said the circus whistled the dogs into a crate the last thing when they left a town, and that every town added a number of animals to the lot. It might have been.

This circus also had a lovely creature who rode on a white horse in the ring, and turned all manner of cartwheels and things, and the morning she came about 15 of us boys went around behind the wagons and watched her take a bath in a canvas bucket. She talked to us while she was doing it, and said this circus was a Hell of an outfit, and she was good and sick of it, and she'd like to know if any of us had any "maws" who were good cooks and would like to see a hungry circus rider eat about two bushels at one session. My mother was always a great hand to deplore public ablutions, and she said there wasn't a chance, but Neil Brandon's mother had a soft spot in her heart because she once swallowed swords in a circus herself, and she had this woman down to eat and Neil probably hasn't got over it yet. I have heard since that circus folks are practically home-bodies, and are quiet and moral, and would be on a par with anybody. But this bareback rider was a little too tough to take, and everybody said it was a good thing when she finally left town. We had her around for a week or so, and I wouldn't wonder if the women thought up excuses to keep their men home during that time.

But she could ride a horse all right. She would practice all morning around and around inside the tent, but she wouldn't perform at the scheduled time because they weren't paying her. Nobody was taking up any admission anyway, so there wasn't any great difference that we could see, except that when we went in the morning we could also watch her take a bath in a canvas bucket. One by one the people who had made up the circus wandered away. Everything was attached and notices posted, so the whole circus was there without many people. A few loyal people stayed on to console the aggrieved owner, among them the lady who bathed in a pail and the man who had the 35 dogs.

There wasn't one of those dogs that was worth having around. They were short-haired, and wouldn't have been able to stand our winter, and they were all little. We are great people for dogs you can see without squinting, and a long-eared hound is about as good as anything except a collie. These little dogs could walk on their front legs, and sit up by the hour, and fetch and carry, and play dead, and run across a wire, and do all manner of little things, but we asked the man if they could run rabbits, and he said he was afraid not. He said they were very valuable dogs, and he had been offered a good deal for them by a number of jealous people who wanted to put him out of business. We asked him why he didn't sell one of them and buy a ticket to Utica, N. Y., and he asked us how much we'd offer, but he didn't get any offers. During the day he would have the dogs on a platform making them practice, and we watched to see what he did, and then we'd go home and train our own dogs to do the same things.

Peter Penley had a big shaggy dog that he taught to walk on his front legs with his hind ones folded up in the air, and Peter's father came home from fishing the next week and saw the dog doing it, and fainted. Of course, every dog in town visited a good deal with the circus dogs, and the man said he wished we'd keep our dogs home. We hadn't ever realized that it was possible to keep a dog home, as our dogs were never tied. We came to the opinion that this man didn't really know much about dogs.

The lion roared all the time, and people said he had the mange. It was quite a circus, and we boys swung on the trapezes and walked on the tight wires, and even rode on the white horse when the woman would let us. After a week or so the man who owned it found some money somewhere, and came back and got us all to help him take the circus down. We took the circus down, and after it was all packed in the wagons, this woman was sitting on a stool out in the middle of the field taking a bath, and half the town was standing around watching her, and then she got dressed and they drove off. Where the elephant had been all the time, there was a pile of manure, and for the next ten years you could see the spot because the witchgrass was about eleven feet high and very rank. It didn't amount to much, I suppose, but at least it gave us an insight into circuses so that none of us ever had a yen to run away with one. I have seen the big circuses that make such a splurge in these later days, and I've never looked at a woman on a white horse but I wondered if she could bathe in a pail. I also recall the remark of Cap'n Winslow Otis, who looked at the ropes and rigging in the big top, and announced that he could fly the whole business with 17 fewer lines. The outside world always had a tough time measuring up in our town.

NOT long ago a professor out in Ohio said country people were mostly foolish, and the only true intellectuals left are city dwellers, which is important if true and will no doubt cheer up a lot of city folks who didn't know it. As one of the measuring sticks of this kind of a survey is always the number of suicides per annum per 1,000 population, it occurred to me that I should study the mental condition of my little town during my youth, and I am glad to report we had two suicides. That probably proves something to professors. Actually, I think those two are the only suicides we ever had in my town from first to last, and in a way I doubt if they should go down into the tabulated statistics without some word of explanation, because they weren't exactly the common run of suicides. I don't know that my town ever had a murder, as such, although I remember a man died once as the result of a fight. Infection set in, they said, and where he was thrown against the barbed wire he got enough infection to take him off. The fight was one of the tail-end frolics at a clambake enjoyed by a group of men who had a barrel of cider in the back of the wagon, and they had held a number of such clambakes in their time without any infection before. There was some talk of arresting the man who threw him against the barbed wire, but as this fellow was not over-popular, a number of claimants came forward, and it wasn't easy to find out who actually did it. The matter was dropped, and the infection was eventually accepted as pretty much so.

But we did have two suicides. The first one was Mel Sternley, who was a great hand to "dwell" on things. One day he went up attic and placed the muzzle of a double-barreled shotgun between his lips, and succeeded in adjusting the triggers so the thing went off. It was a 12-gauge shotgun, and it took out a hole in the roof about the size of a clam basket. Mr. Sternley, it was announced around the community, had taken his life, although the local paper tempered the report of his demise out of respect for the feelings of the family, and said he "died suddenly Tuesday."

Our other suicide was a much better story, and was chronicled minutely by papers as far away as New York, although some of the more minute details escaped Pothead Bibber and me at the time. We saw it. Pothead and I were sitting on Featherwhite Wharf catching sculpins. We weren't trying to catch sculpins, and I never knew of anybody who did try to catch them, but that's what we were catching. We were trying to catch some harbor pollock, which is a more desirable fish. And while we were sitting there we looked up and saw Ross McIver's Model T truck coming down over the hill onto the wharf. Ross and Mrs. McIver were sitting up in the cab as if they were out for a Sunday afternoon drive. There was nothing unusual in Ross's coming down to the wharf, because he did trucking, and at least twice a day he'd come down to pick up or leave things at boat time. So we kept fishing. And Ross came down over the hill with his truck, and drove out onto the wharf, and kept right on going, and drove off over the end of the wharf into the harbor.

I don't know how anybody else would have responded, but Pothead and I didn't do anything. We sat there with the lines in our hands pretty much as if we saw trucks drive off the end of the wharf every fifteen minutes or so, and then we looked at each other, and Pothead said, "That was Ross McIver." Now, at the time, this sounded like a perfectly intelligent remark, and Pothead's tone of voice suggested he was giving me ample opportunity to dispute his statement if I saw fit. But I knew it was Ross, because it was his truck that went into the river, and we'd both seen Ross driving it and his wife sitting beside him. It took at least as long as this for us to get into action, and then we took a turn around two spiles with our fish lines, and ran over and looked into the water. We couldn't see anything. It was high water slack, and our harbor was always milky from the flats, but I guess we couldn't have seen anything anyway, because there was water enough there to take any vessel afloat. So we ran up to the store and told them Ross McIver had just driven his truck off the end of the wharf, and at first nobody believed us. "What would he do that for?" old Cap'n Parker said. But after a while people went down, and they could see the place where the planking was ripped as the truck tipped down over, and they poked down with a long gaff and said they could hit something. They swung out the fish hoist and tried to catch a hook on something, but it was almost low water before they finally got a hitch. Then they found the hoist wasn't stout enough to bring the truck up, and there was a lot of running around. "Stuck in the mud," they said. Everybody in town was on the wharf by then, and somebody strung up a rope for them to stand behind. Some men came over from the shipyard with heavy gear, and they rigged a shears with some spar timbers and finally got the truck up. I remember they miscalculated on the hoist, and the blocks came together before the truck was out of the water. They slung chains to it and made a new hitch. Some of the women made sandwiches and brought down coffee, and Pothead and I ate a lot of the sandwiches and drank a good bit of coffee along with the men. A lot of the women spoke to us kindly, and said what an awful thing it was that we'd seen such a thing, but Pothead and I thought it was pretty lucky we happened to be there, or nobody would have known where to look for the McIvers. The medical examiner, who was just Dr. Pillsbury, pronounced death due to drowning, and they took up the McIvers in big baskets and took them home. Pothead and I went home then, too, and had to tell everybody over and over again how the thing happened.

But naturally we didn't know how the thing happened. Down at the wharf everybody thought it had been an accident, and a number of people said Ross must have had a stroke. But Dr. Pillsbury said he didn't have any stroke. Tinker-Bob Jordan looked the truck over and said the brakes were all right. There weren't any brake marks on the wharf, though. Seemed to be a very curious thing. But later on the real story came out.

The truth was that Mrs. McIver had a cancer. She felt bad all the time, and tried as hard as could be not to show it. She wouldn't give in. Ross knew all about it, and tried to get her to take things slower, and not to be working so hard. But Mrs. McIver wasn't that kind of a woman. Ross himself was as healthy as a trout, and he was always telling the other men how inconsiderate he was of his wife. He seemed to think his own strength and health was unfair to Mrs. McIver, and things got him down after a while. He just figured it would be the humane thing to end the whole affair. Of course, all this came out afterwards when people began piecing things together and remembering what Ross and his wife had said at this time and that time. That morning, when Ross must have made up his mind to drive himself and his wife into the harbor, she was working in the kitchen. Her sink still had dirty dishes in it, and everybody knew Mrs. McIver would never have knowingly gone off to her death with a sink full of dishes. She wouldn't have gone anyway and left them, but she certainly wouldn't have left them if she'd known what he was up to. She had a pie half made on the kitchen shelf, and a cake in the oven. People figured she hadn't the faintest notion what he had in mind. He must have come in and said, "Come quick, May, see what's going on at the wharf!" Must have been that way, because she didn't have a hat on, and was still wearing her apron.

People talked about how she must have felt when she got to the wharf and looked up at her husband—him staring straight ahead and not a word out of him. People wondered if she had time to figure the thing out—if she thought he was just plain crazy, or if understanding suddenly came to her and she knew. Pothead and I, in the two days after that, heard all this talk, and realized there was a good deal more to the affair than what we had seen. On the third day we went down and stood on the other side of the street and watched when the funeral was held, and I think both of us realized at that time that people sometimes do things that other folks don't understand.

ONE time Ed Hale swapped a barrel of vinegar with
Nathan Foster for credit on his grocery bill, and then Ed
told all around town how he'd put one over on Nate.
Nate wasn't any the wiser, but the truth was that the
barrel wasn't vinegar at all. It wasn't old enough to be
vinegar. It was just good hard cider, and Ed's hard cider
had a reputation for reliability. Thus it happened that
several men about the village began to think of ways and
means of investigating the basement of Nate Foster's general store, and it didn't take long to arrive at a plan.

Jim Thatcher came in first and said, "Nate, mind if I
use the toilet?" Nate, busy weighing out something at the
grocery counter, said, "Nope—downstairs, light button's
by the top step." So Jim went down and made a quick
hunt and located the barrel, horsed up along with several
other barrels, but not yet fitted with a spigot. Then he
flushed the toilet and came back up and went out.

You can't hurry a thing like that, so they waited two days before Harry Jameson came in with a bit and bit-brace under his coat and a spigot in his pocket. He inquired if he might use the facilities, and he quickly put the spigot in the barrel, flushed the toilet, and returned to the upper level. After that every man in town, almost, was carrying a glass or a tin cup in his pocket, and would go in every now and then to use Nate's toilet. Nate observed the popularity of the plumbing, and said, "You'd think nobody else in town had a hopper," but he didn't know about the cider and made no deductions. Things went along for a couple of weeks or so, and John Baker kind of gave the thing away. He came in all of a tear and rushed down cellar, and was hardly up and out again before he returned. On his third visit, Nate looked up and said, "If you're as bad off as that, should think you'd stay to home and play safe," to which John replied, with a fairly thick voice, "I forgot to flush, they tol' me not to forget to flush." This he dutifully did, and bumped into a display of tinware on his way out, and people figured from then on Nate must have thought something was going on.

The next morning a half dozen men were standing on Nate's doorstep when he came in at six o'clock to open up the store, and they rushed down cellar in a body and came up again in a few minutes after only flushing once. Nate said afterward he suspicioned something, and went down after they came up and looked all around, but he didn't see anything, and thought he'd go down with the next one who came in and keep an eye peeled. But the next one who came in was Judge Proctor.

Our judge was given to cider himself, although it had to be good cider, and whenever complaints were lodged with him by the local W. C. T. U. he made a point of conducting the investigation himself. That morning a complaint had been lodged that Nate Foster was selling liquor.

One of the temperance leaders had the story from somebody who talked with the road crew in the gravel pit, and the road crew had been definitely tipsy on duty, and things had come to a pretty pass. Judge Proctor came in and said to Nate, "Nate, where's your cider?"

Nate, still not suspecting anything, made an honest reply and said, "Over back of the nail kegs, in under the counter, I'll get a glass." So he pulled out a keg of nails and brought out a glass jug of very good cider, and he and the judge tested it for body, flavor, and also spirituous content, and decided it was good. Judge Proctor said, "How much of it you got?"

"Just that," said Nate, "I didn't make any last fall, and Hod Peabody gave me a jugful for Christmas. Have another?"

The judge had another, and said he'd had a complaint Nate was selling drinks. Nate said he hadn't sold any, but he'd like to buy some, as he hadn't been able this winter to shout people to a boiled owl when they paid their bills Saturday night, and a lot of people spoke of it. The investigation wasn't making much headway when in came little Peewee Thurston on the dead run, making as if he was unbuttoning his clothes, and he popped down the cellar stairs. That put Nate in mind of his suspicions about carryings-on down cellar, and he popped down right after Peewee and caught him drawing off a dipper. The story came out after that, and everybody had a good laugh. The cider was almost all gone by the time Nate found out. Some people said that the W. C. T. U. woman went by Nate's just as Judge Proctor stepped out about noontime, and the Judge stopped her and said the whole thing was a trumped-up falsification, and it never did happen, and Nate was an honest man, and that on account of malicious misinformation a horrible mistake had come within an ace of taking place. He explained to her that a miserable distemper was going the rounds, and that it left people weak in the knees and recurred without warning, often many times a day, and that Mr. Foster had not been selling liquor, but was on the contrary an upright man who had kindly opened his plumbing facilities in this emergency. "In fact," said the judge, "Mr. Foster's kindness has been at great expense to himself, and I doubt if his water bill this quarter will run much under forty dollars."

The reason so many people heartily enjoyed this story was because Nate was, himself, the town's biggest practical joker, and hardly anybody had gone scot-free from some of his schemes. I was all of ten when I was in there one day to get Mother some pickling spice, and Nate was measuring out some yard goods for a woman. I was by the big window, because the grocery counter was in that end, and I saw Bill Belcher coming up the street. Bill was a combination cattle trader, horse jockey, butcher, and veterinarian, and was always drunk except when he went away every few months to take the Keeley cure. He was drunk that day, and although it was late summer, he had on his buffalo fur coat. That, however, was nothing strange, any more than a straw hat in January. Bill reached for the hook in the hall when he went out by, and what he got was what he wore.

Nate, cutting yard goods, also saw Bill, and he vaulted over the counter, sprinted the length of the store, scooped up an egg from the crate by the window, kicked open the screen door, and let the egg fly in the direction of Bill. By the time it hit Bill, Nate was back with his yard goods again.

It hit Bill right on the ear, and lacking any definite information about who had perpetrated this outrage, Bill began a systematic program of retaliation that involved everybody on the street. His passage from in front of Nate's to the postoffice was a whirlwind of mayhem, and included the Unitarian minister who had just stepped out of the postoffice with his arms full of Sunday School papers. Art Fuller put an end to it by clipping Bill, and Bill and the minister lay side by side on the sidewalk for ten or fifteen minutes.

I was standing in the window watching all these people picking themselves up, and almost jumped out of my overalls when Nate said to me, most calmly, "And now, young man, what can I do you for?"

"Stuff for pickles," was all I could remember.

Nate put me up a bag of spice packages, and said, "Tell your ma not to forget to put in cucumbers. I had pickles once the woman left out cukes, and they don't make much of a hit." Not a word about that egg!

And do you want to know something? I was the only person in town besides Nate and that woman buying cloth who knew what happened that day. Nate is dead, and he never told anybody. The woman moved away, and I don't know that she did. And a lot of people in my town are going to learn right here and now, for the first time, just what made Bill Belcher hit the Unitarian minister. It may not be important, but at least there are some things go on in a small town that aren't blabbed about for the sake of talk.

Another time I went into Nate's store, and he was up on a nail keg poking a yardstick through a hole in the wall plaster up near the ceiling. He got down, hung the yardstick on a nail, and waited on me. That's all I knew about it at the time, but I got the rest of the story later. Next door to Nate's was a restaurant, and Martha Maynard did the cooking. She was a good cook, and everything she served was just like home. Her can of cream-tartar was up on a shelf, and one day years back Nate had carefully dug a small hole through the partition wall so he could poke her can of cream-tartar off with his yardstick. He had a hole in the end of the stick, and drove in a brad to hang it handy. Two or three times a day he'd poke the stick through the hole and knock down the can. Of course, two or three times a day Martha would come by that way and find her can of cream-tartar on the floor, and she'd pick it up and set it back on the shelf. And that went on for years and years. Everybody in town knew about Nate's trick, and not a soul ever told Martha. Martha never said anything about it, and there never was any indication that she suspected foul play. I wouldn't mention it here now, except that Martha isn't around—she went to her grave unenlightened, and that is the way it should have been.

Some of Nate's jokes required so much preparation that the end result was never worth it. I know about one time a woman asked him for special cuts of steak, because she was having company that counted. Nate cut them off for her, and took them out back to wrap, and that evening at supper time the woman opened the package, her frying pan red hot on the stove, and found she had a half dozen bananas instead of steaks. And it wasn't more than a minute of what-shall-I-do's when a knock came to the back door, and there was Nate apologizing all over the piazza and handing her the steaks as if a horrible mistake had been made. Some people claimed Nate must have stood outside the window just to see what the woman did, but we don't know. At least he walked a half-mile to deliver the steaks at the split-second moment, and he must have had a pleasant afternoon dwelling in his own mind on the sunken-feeling that woman was going to have. Reward is elusive. And the woman knew Nate well enough not to imagine the "mistake" had been anything but a put-up job.

Nobody will ever know how many things Nate engineered that were never traced to him. He had the handles from a trolley car nailed to the wall in his store office. He got them off a Boston Elevated car. The motorman stepped away from his controls for a minute, for something, and Nate pocketed the control handles and moved back in the car. Alongside the handles, nailed on the wall, was a framed clipping from the Boston Globe telling about this traffic tie-up in Park Street subway because somebody stole the control handles.

Nate used to put posters in his store window advertising local functions. All the stores did that. When you were on the advertising committee for a high school play, or anything like that, you would make up a lot of posters, and would ask the storekeepers if you could put them in the windows. Nate naturally put in a poster one time for a big event which was wholly in his own imagination, and quite a crowd turned out to find the hall locked and dark. Not so often, after that, did people use his window for posters—we had a feeling less whimsical storekeepers were a safer advertising medium.

Nate had been to sea as a boy, and came home with enough money to live on the rest of his days. He set up the store to give himself something to do, and he never insisted that it do any more than pay for itself. I don't know how the tax experts would look at that kind of a business today. You're supposed to show at least some intention of making a profit. Nate did make a profit, and a good one, but he never had that as a basic purpose, and once in a while he would sell things so far below cost that it would make tears come to your eyes. It was always to embarrass a "competitor." Once a competitor put in some new models of a kitchen range, and for some reason no lid lifters came with them. He had a stick he kept by the display, for lifting the lids, and with short-sighted explanation he made the remark, "The lid lifter comes extra." Nate got hold of that, and he went to the city and bought up all the lid lifters he could find and piled them in his front window with a sign that read, "Cornered the market." It must have cost him something, and the only fun he got out of it after the first go-off was to run a sale every year on lid lifters. I suppose two dozen lid lifters is more than my town bought in a hundred years, if they bought anywhere near that many, and Nate had hundreds of them.

Another time our drugstore made a springtime window display of patent medicines. Everybody who could grow a beard, in those days, got out a bottle of cure-all with his picture on the label, and as the concoctions were largely edible alcohol, there was a certain popularity to the things. Nate saw the display, and immediately fixed up a window. All he had in the window was a jug of molasses and a glass jar of yellow sulphur. A sign stated that Old Doctor Nathan Foster's sure-fire remedy for that spring sluggishness had never been improved upon, and anybody buying a dollar's worth of groceries could have a dose free. And don't worry—a good many people had a free dose, because sulphur and molasses were believed in staunchly, and still are, and what you believe in is half the battle. It was such a good stunt Nate repeated it annually ever afterward—even into the not-so-latter days when sulphur and molasses had no prestige at all and vitamin pills were coming into favor.

Merle Blake, our spiritualistic mail man, naturally kept two good horses and was a great hand for remedies for this and that. At one time he owned a black pacing mare who had raced as Fancy Free, and held eight world's records when she came of age. I don't know what those records were, and sometimes a World's Record is nothing but making the New Gloucester track in 2.10, but whatever her records were, she held them. She also had worms. Merle spent a good part of his time exercising Fancy Free and treating her for her unfortunate malady. It was a custom in the town to think of things which sounded like treatments for worms, and to pass these remedies on with corroborative evidence to Merle, who would then try them on Fancy Free and report, in due time, that they didn't work. This made it essential to think up a new remedy, and one of the saddest lapses of recorded history is that nobody ever compiled a list of all the things Merle did to cure Fancy Free of the worms.

Fancy Free was a beautiful mare, and her foals were always salable. It seemed a shame to me, as a boy, that a creature so beautiful should go through life under such a wretched handicap. We all thought the same, and we never saw Merle anywhere but we boys would dutifully inquire as to Fancy Free's condition, whereupon Merle would go into details and shake his head and cluck through his teeth. I was at least 19 or 20 before I found out that Fancy Free not only had the worms no longer, but never had any at all, and our spiritualistic mail man was the victim of one of Nate Foster's jokes. It seems Merle, who knew all things by virtue of short and effective trances, had never thought to have one over Fancy Free's worms, and had gone through life the victim of a hoax.

Soon after he got Fancy Free, Merle took her to the farrier's to have her shoes changed, and Nate happened in on his way back from a trip up Stinking Brook to show what he'd caught just as the blacksmith was working on Fancy Free. Nate knocked his leftover angle worms out of a Prince Albert can at the time, and they dropped behind Fancy Free and distributed themselves around on top of what they dropped on. The blacksmith said, "Sure as Hell, Merle'll treat her for worms if he sees that." It was then but a matter of casual comment to make sure that Merle did see it, and Merle sucked through his teeth and oh-deared, and led Fancy Free off up home the way people get taken to the hospital. Her treatment dated from then on.

It was necessary, after that, for Nate to sneak into Merle's stable a couple of times a week and throw a few worms on the manure behind Fancy Free, and in order to do this during the colder months, it was necessary for Nate to undertake the culture of worms. He was able, sometimes, to get worms from the beds in the greenhouse, but Oscar Gamble, the florist, wouldn't let him dig sometimes when it might disturb plantings, so Nate fixed up a bed of his own behind the furnace, and always had plenty of worms to take up and leave in Merle's stable. Nobody ever pointed out to Merle that horses have worms other than those used for fishing purposes, and for some reason he never stumbled on that fact, in spite of his powers to read the past and foretell the future with great accuracy. Fancy Free was a patient animal.

I wouldn't want to leave Nate Foster as if his whole life had been devoted to playing. He was a good man, and was more than respected by all. He played a big part in governing our town, and did a great many charitable acts. He was one of the men my father always suspected when he went, as church treasurer, to pay the coal bill for the church, and the coal man said, "That's been paid for, here's your receipt." A man who will do things like that can be spotted a few moments of pleasure if, as they sometimes did, they irk folks. And even if they irk some folks, those moments certainly mean a lot in later life to lads like myself who grew up during them. I might not be able to put my finger on the everlasting values, but I know I'm glad I saw Nate throw that egg, even if the Unitarian minister finds my joy distasteful.

ONCE a year we had a merchants' picnic. It came on Wednesday, because Wednesday was always a half holiday in the stores anyway, and the merchants could thus put on a picnic and lose only the forenoon. I forget just when the merchants stopped putting on this celebration, but it must have been around 1920 or so, and the cessation wasn't mourned as much then as I mourn it now. Those were before the days of Chambers of Commerce, and it wasn't necessary to carry on a big preparation program to get the town united on a worth-while project. All they ever did was announce the day, and the entire town turned out for the event from the little ones who were still nursing to the antique Grand Army veterans.

The clam chowder was made in a big galvanized boiler on wheels, a contraption made by Willie Monroe for the purpose. It was square cornered, and the size of a modern gasoline truck—well, a small one. The wheels were from old mowing machines, being steel they wouldn't burn, and the chowder was made by pulling the tank of ingredients over a good fire. They stoked under the tank, and every little while Maynard Garrison would climb up on a step on the back end and peer in to see if the thing was progressing according to schedule. Maynard was the best chowder maker in the world, and he could turn out a little one for two people on a stove just as well as he could make 300 gallons for the merchants' picnic. He would stand up on the step with a long handled spoon and taste and test, and then climb back to the ground with a satisfied look. The people who were lined up with their bowls, and sometimes with ten quart pails, silently worshiped Maynard in an awed way, and he could have been elected to any office in Maine. When he finally gave the signal, they took the tongue of the chowder boiler, and pulled it off from the fire, and the entire town sat down at once, simultaneously, to a piping hot clam chowder. The gods on Olympus must have come down on those Wednesdays to join, incognito, in the feast. The clams had been dug that morning, less than hours before the time to eat, and the juice of the North Atlantic still coursed in their veins as they mingled and mixed with the gastric juices. The best was none too good for Maynard, and he was particular about whose milk he used, and who grew the onions, and even about who cut up the potatoes. The potatoes had to be cut right.

One year a fellow happened through town, and he thought the chowder was good, and when he got back to his home in the city somewhere he told a household editor on a newspaper about the wonderful chowder he had up in Maine, and this editor wrote to Maynard and asked him for his receet. Maynard sent it. It was his Merchants' Picnic receet, and it started with forty gallons of clam broth, 150 gallons of milk, seven barrels of clams (more or less), and 300 pounds of potatoes. Maynard asked to have a clipping sent to him, as he didn't see that paper ordinarily, but he never got one. We used to laugh about it, thinking of city people in their snug little homes trying to make one of Maynard's chowders on a gas stove. It takes about 15 acres of shoreland to stage one of Maynard's chowders.

We also had steamed clams on these picnics. And lobsters. There was always an undercurrent of opinion that the storekeepers saved themselves a lot of lobsters by filling everybody with clams and chowder first, but this was hardly true, because any Maine town is composed, at least 50%, of people who can always eat a lobster no matter what has gone before. The pile of lobsters on the shore, waiting for the pit to get hot, was something a boy never forgets, even if the passage of time may magnify it. It was certainly head-high to us at the time, even if the record isn't clear as to just how high our heads reached in those days. The pit where they were to be steamed was just a place where rocks had been laid in against a ledge, and a hardwood fire was burned on it during the forenoon. The rocks got hot. Awful hot. About the time the chowder was ready, Mike Thatcher would take a garden rake and pull all the remains of the fire to one side, and then they'd toss in the lobsters. Everybody tossed lobsters. When the first one was tossed a great hiss of steam went up into the sky, and we cheered. It didn't take long to pile them up on the hot rocks, and then they threw on a big wad of rockweed, and pulled a sailcloth on over the rockweed to keep the steam in. It takes about 45 minutes that way, maybe an hour, and is just long enough to see to the chowder.

The steamed clams used to be done in an old bathtub. They plugged up the drainhole and set the tub across a rock arch. The bottom of the tub would get red hot, and the first year they used it, all the enamel peeled off inside and out. After the clams were put in, they'd lay old newspapers over the top, several thicknesses, to keep in the steam, and it was a kind of a tradition in our town that Martin Holman was privileged to burn his fingers finding out if the clams were done. He burned himself every year, in full view of the crowd, and everybody stood around waiting to hear him swear. He would tear a little hole in the soggy newspapers on top of the tub, being most dainty about it, because the paper was hot, and then he would break through the last layer of paper. The impounded steam, enough to pull all the trains in Maine for a week, would assist him in rending this last covering. The burst of steam would come rousting out and envelop Martie, and proceed onward and upward jubilantly into the farthest regions of space. Martie would jump back like a pig that's hit an electric fence, and make harangue in the most magnificent language. It was a ritual, sort of. He still had to fish out a clam from the top of the tub, see if it had opened its secret wonder to the curious eyes of the famished, and taste it carefully. Then they would rip off the newspapers, bring up a big wooden bowl, and scoop out clams for anybody who held his dish up.

People brought lunches, besides. The merchants didn't supply everything to eat. They were family lunches, to be laid out on a blanket around which the family circled. Coffee was made by the merchants, in wash boilers horsed in tandem on still another adequate fire. The main principle connected with coffee making in those days was to use a good bit of coffee, and to boil it until the essence was extracted and left saturating the liquid. It would, I suppose, float an egg. It might even have floated a spike. It certainly was good, and my generation knew what coffee was. Coffee made like that wants to boil up twice, good. You let it boil up once, and set it off the fire. It will swirl and seethe, but it won't roll out over the edge. After it has settled a mite, it wants to be set back on the fire again, and allowed to boil up good a second time. Then, just before it mounts out over the sides, you want to splash into it about a quart of cold water right out of the well. That prompts the coffee grounds to give up, and they settle to the bottom of the boiler and leave the amber as clear as any crystal. Hap Peters always made our coffee in my time, and referred to it as ambrosial elixir.

One year, during the sugar shortage, people didn't have anything to sweeten their coffee, and that was the year Vance MacVitty, our barber, brought sugar for everybody. He'd been hoarding sugar, and being a barber on the main street but not strictly a merchant, he had something of a half-caste connection with the picnic. That year he brought a firkin full of sugar, and he sat on a stool with it on his knees, and anybody who wanted sugar went and helped himself.

The sports in the afternoon were designed to give everybody something to do. We always had a ball game between the high school team and a special team of women. The women were all good players, and we had one girl, Doris Macomber, who could pitch good enough for the leagues. The high school boys all played left-handed, or right if they were southpaws, and the game was something to see. There was also a game between our own Townies and the team from the next town. That was the game that the men all bet on, and it was common knowledge that $100 would bring down the best pitcher of either the Braves or the Red Sox for the day, and it was also common knowledge that our home-town boys could frequently knock them off the diamond.

One year the next town showed up with a stranger in their midst, and he had arms like dory sweeps and stood about ten feet high. He warmed up in full view of everybody, and was most impressive. They said afterward he was a professional from New York, and led his league the year before, and had a no-hit record as good as most. He did, however, make the mistake of enjoying too much picnic before the game, and he turned out to be logey. Dannie Shaw, our left fielder, was first up for our team, and he picked off the first fast ball as neat as Mother hitting a wasp on the kitchen window with a copy of the New England Homestead, and sailed it out into the sparkling blue flood tide of the Atlantic Ocean and went around the bases tipping his hat to everybody. The trained-seal pitcher blew up on the next man, and then our team's manager went over and asked Doris Macomber if she'd like to pinch-hit. Doris was as pretty as a pail of new milk, and she stepped up to the plate and spit on her hands and pawed the ground with her left foot, and indicated where she'd like to have one—about so high and just a hair outside—and she brought the bat back and looked about as formidable as nothing at all. The crowd quieted down so we could hear the waves lapping on the rocks below the clam boiler, and the hot-shot pitcher from New York wound up as if he was flailing beans, and put the ball right where Doris had asked. By the time it got to Doris the man on first was half-way to third, and Doris cut the ball over to first with a good clip. It hit the ground two or three times on the way out, and the man on first fielded it neatly and heaved it to third. The man on third caught it prettily, made no effort to tag the runner, and tossed it to first. Then the firstbaseman threw it to home plate, because the runner was going that way, fast, and the catcher got it too late to make any important contribution with it, and all he could think of to do was throw it to first and intercept Doris if possible. After that they threw the ball around a good deal, and Doris finally scored on what Artie Brown, our official scorer, officially chalked up as "fielders whimsey."

There was a good deal of complaint from the visiting team about the play, it being contended by the manager that Doris was not a member of the team. This was hardly tenable, inasmuch as Doris was in uniform from the previous game, and it was the same uniform, and the crowd appeared mostly to disagree. Our umpire, who was a good one, was old Bill Toothaker, who stuttered. It was a local claim that Bill had been known to call out, "S-s-s-s-Ball one!", but I never heard him do it, myself. He said he didn't find anything in the rules, or in the ground regulations, that prevented Doris from taking part, and that personally he thought it was a m-m-m-m-ost remarkable demonstration of b-b-baseb-b-ball, and that was that, and "Play Ball!" So we played, and our team drove the New Yorker from the box in two innings, and the neighboring town reverted to their own man, and they caught up in the sixth, and trimmed us 13-12. To give the New Yorker his due, however, everybody admitted the lobsters and clams were what slowed him up. The way he ate, you'd think he never saw food before. We found out afterward he cost our neighbors $300, and he was paid off without being requested to come again. In those days we didn't go to Boston much to see ball games.

The horseshoe pitching contest was usually won by Herman Potter, who pitched horseshoes all summer in his back yard, and then moved down cellar and pitched all winter. He could win a game with seven ringers, and usually did. This made it far more significant, in our town, to win second, and it was my fame one year to win it. I had good luck, and a little twist that Herman showed me. The prizes for all the contests were donated by the merchants, and so nobody would feel hurt, there were lollypops and chocolate creams for all the children who competed but didn't win in the three-legged race, the potato race, or the broad jump. We all had fun.

The attendance thinned out after the ball games, and we were always home before dark. The merchants used to pay Honey-Boy Broderick five dollars to clean up the grounds and burn the papers and things, and some of the boys now and then stayed after dark to help him. It was said they always found some money around, that people had lost. Then there were the sody-bottles to redeem, and on top of everything else, there was the grand bonfire on the beach after dark—with the rips singing their night song on the flats, and the lighthouses blinking in from outside, and flocks of ducks talking to themselves as they fed in on the tide, and the stars standing just above the tops of the oaks that fringed the banks. It was something like the long ago, when the Indians sat there the same way, with a fire, and tossed their clamshells off over the bank. Honey-Boy they said, told some good stories, but Honey-Boy wasn't supposed to be altogether bright, and some of us weren't allowed to remain for this aftermowing of a busy day.

It was just as well, probably, because the night was more likely than not a restless time, and some of us got good doses of castor "ile" in case, and those of us who didn't would have been better off if we had, and there was a general belief about that time that everybody in town had eaten altogether too much.

And so we had, but if the merchants of my town should suddenly announce a revival of this neglected antiquity, I would be the first to promise to go, and I would gladly eat too much all over again.

OUR town still kept up its contacts by water with the great outside world. It was wholly a tribute to a wonderful past, because if you wanted to get anywhere the trains and the highways offered superior accommodations. We still had a number of people, however, who always went down to the harbor and made their trips with Cap'n Newcomb. Partly, no doubt, it was a gesture to keep Cap'n Newcomb happy, although it is equally likely that our folks preferred the water under any circumstances to overland transportation at its best. There was supposed to be a schedule for the boat, but along at the last of it Cap'n Newcomb would take you about anywhere you wanted to go, and would sometimes wait around to bring you home again.

Cap'n Newcomb was another of our old timers who had cut his teeth on a taffrail, and had retired after years at sea to let his arteries harden in a drier air. But after the cuffs on his pants dried out, he decided he'd had enough of shore life, and he went back to sea and skippered the ancient Lalage. The Lalage was the white-painted steamer that had grown decrepit in the island run, and long after any real need of her had vanished, she still puffed around the bay and gave Cap'n Newcomb an excuse to haunt the salt water. She was supposed to run into Portland at stated intervals, but I don't know that she did. In the first of my being around, the Lalage "went three." "We go three" means a skipper, cook and engineer; although along the Maine coast the engineer sometimes bakes the best bread, and the cook may do the real navigating. The Lalage was named by some coastal classicist who knew his Horace, but his public twisted the name to "Lallygag." Everybody knew that Lalage was a young lady out of a poem, but nobody would dignify her. The Lallygag fortunately had a mail contract, and the super-efficiency of the Post Office department had a lot to do with her being in service in my time. Cap'n Newcomb was always going around with a petition to sign, which he would forward to the Postmaster General to frustrate the claims of the railroad that the mail could be handled more expeditiously by train. Everybody signed the captain's petitions, and nobody would have offended him for the world. I suppose it was nice to have those days—when nobody's business was so important that split-second mail service was considered a good thing. The Post Office Department must have felt the petitions were imposing, because Cap'n Newcomb carried the mail for a long time into the age of speed, and some days we wouldn't get any mail at all if he decided to lay in somewhere and line up a cribbage game. Long after other communities were delighted with regularity of mail delivery, Cap'n Newcomb was poking up the harbor with our mail. He still had the contract almost up to the time he fell off the fire station roof one day, while helping to lay shingles, and broke his neck. He was eighty-something. The Lallygag lay at the wharf for a time, but never went to sea again, and then she was towed out to the seaward shore of Big Muffin Island and beached. What's left of her lays there today if you care to go and look.

Back along, there had been an active and busy corporation known as The Boston and Maritime Seaboard Private Lines. Nobody ever found out what was private about them. In the long ago, the company had operated sloops out of Newburyport, and coasted down to Maine for whatever business turned up. When steamers came along, they had a number like the Lalage, running about 100 feet. The freight and passengers mingled cozily, and it was distinctly a treat of real beauty to enjoy a quiet ride in and out of the islands and coves of the coast. The Lalage once gave our town regular service in and out, back when the ocean was the highway and the people were tidal minded. I suppose the skippers of these craft were the most seawise of any who ever sailed. The Gulf of Maine with its inlets and outlets, sounds and cuts, reaches and rocks, bars and shoals, where the tides run high, wide and handsome, offers navigation problems other parts of the world have missed. Those fellows, like our lobstermen today, would compute the wind and tide, and bring their vessel in over a knife-edge reef so the keel would just bruise the rockweed—and they'd never look down. Two minutes' difference of the tide would have left them a stranded wreck. They knew when to come in over, and when to go around, all the way from Block Island to Cape Breton Island, and if you can do that you can sail anything anywhere. Cap'n Newcomb was like those old skippers, except that he came later, and he had to make up in tradition and glory what he lacked in freight and passengers.

But he didn't take his steamboating too seriously. He knew he was licked, and he wasn't trying to save a gone goose. The ten gauge shotgun in his pilothouse was for waterfowling, and many a time the Lalage wouldn't show up until long after dark because Cap'n Newcomb had gone gunning. Passengers, if any, had no vote in the decisions. If geese were available, Cap'n Newcomb would decide to go goosing, and if the passengers were the fretting type, they fretted while he went. Mostly, though, passengers joined in, and many a 20¢ ticket bought a traveler some rare sport, even if he was late at arriving. Many a night we would be around the wharf, and we'd hear the old gun bark and boom down toward Bullhorse Rock, and we'd know Cap'n Newcomb had a raft of geese he was working. One fall morning he took a celebrated cruise, and I had the chance to chew on one of the geese he brought home. That morning some drummers were leaving town on the train, and somebody told them about the Lallygag. They thought it would be a lark, so they piled their sample cases into a wagon and had themselves driven to the wharf. They asked to be taken to Rockland and slapped down the money for their fares.

Cap'n Newcomb was fair about it. He told them he had it in mind to head down Rockland way, but this was the fall of the year. He said the geese and sea ducks were rafting in, and coot were plentiful, and he had it in mind to lay by a few. They might, he said, be delayed somewhat en route. The salesmen were delighted. They had the wagon hurry them back to the village, and they borrowed and hired shotguns, and picked up ammunition. They also picked up a good supply of goosedown solvent, which Ransom's store handled in those days under the name of Dr. Grady's Patent Elixir of Life and Body Builder. The Lallygag tooted, the engine churned, and away they all went on what the Public Utilities Commission accepted as a scheduled accommodation.

Nothing was heard of the Lallygag for three days. Back then the Coast Guard didn't get called in until a man had been given a good chance to show up by himself, so nobody worried. Fishermen all along the coast, later, told how they'd seen the Lallygag, now here and now there. She was usually heading into a raft of geese, whereupon there would be a broadside, and then they'd let down the small boat and pick up what they'd got. They had a pool of $100 up for high man, and Cap'n Newcomb led from the first shot. They put into several places for ammunition and whistle balm, sometimes getting both at one place, and sometimes being unlucky enough as to get only ammunition. The Lallygag had 467 geese when she arrived at Rockland Breakwater, and the salesmen came ashore saying they'd had a wonderful time. Cap'n Newcomb was back in our harbor the next tide but one, and he sent word around for us boys to help him distribute the geese. Not a shred went to waste, and the Baptist Ladies' Aid took all the down and made a comfortable for a poor family. The goose I saved out for our family was large and aged, and was well shot. She was tough and gamey, and Mother told me it wasn't always a good plan to go for the big things.

Once in a great while some irate passenger on this public carrier would complain to the main office that his connections were badly disrupted during the shooting season. The main office no doubt had a form reply, but they were bankrupt anyway and I don't imagine they cared. The company, as such, went out of existence long before Cap'n Newcomb died, and they said he paid out a good deal of his own money to keep the Lallygag afloat. He had his own way of enjoying himself, and a passenger who took time seriously didn't know much about our community.

The Lallygag did figure in a lot of thrilling sea rescues. It seemed as if Cap'n Newcomb had an extra sense about being on hand when a picnic party swamped or somebody piled onto a ledge. He'd come tooting into the harbor with everybody wrapped in blankets, and stand in the pilothouse giving orders until everybody was rescued. Usually the victims were in high spirits and having a good time. The water off Maine is cold, and anybody who has been picked out of it is always so glad that a sort of exhilaration sets in. Cap'n Newcomb's best rescue was the time he picked up Bill Bureau from a watery grave. Bill was a Malaga Islandite who had been put in our town when the state commenced its social uplift work among the offshore underprivileged. He was a nice fellow, and the sea flowed salt brine in his veins from far back when the Portuguese first poked out to see where the ocean went. He got some gasoline in the bilge of his lobster boat, and then when he lit his pipe he discovered it. The next thing he knew he was hugging the bellbuoy at the end of Cooper's Cove Reef, and the wind was blowing up southerly so folks would want their sprayhoods up. Bill was a little groggy from the blast, and his pipe was wet and wouldn't burn, and he slipped his belt through the ring on the buoy, buckled it, and settled down to what comfort he could take as night descended and wrapped him in darkness. This ring on a bellbuoy is so the lighthouse tender can come alongside and hoist the buoy to the deck for repairs. Otherwise the only appurtenances to a bellbuoy are the floating base, made to rock like a roly-poly doll, and the bell which bongs whenever the base rocks. Bellbuoys are designed so they will ring the bell at every opportunity, and run mostly to instability for that reason. The bell is a large bell, with a rich tone that can be heard through a gale at all distances consistent with danger. A southerly wind is considered the most cooperative. So Bill slopped around on the ovoid base with great trust in his belt, and the night passed. He was seasick in about two minutes—him as had rounded the Horn fit and hale a hundred times. In ten minutes he was a raving maniac. He spewed and blew, and his head flew into thousands of granular sparks every time the big clapper came about in the big bell. Day broke, and the day passed. The next day Cap'n Newcomb picked him off, wrapped him in a blanket, and brought him ashore. Bill sat around the rest of his life after that, and all he ever did was jump about six inches off his chair, by day, and his bed by night, whenever his recollective fancy told him the bell had struck again. He never spoke, and he had no reaction whatever from real bells. Church bells on Sunday, or the fire bell, or a train, or striking the ship's bells didn't mean a thing and he didn't show that he heard them, but whenever his numbed brain told him the swell was dipping again, and the clapper was about to clap, he'd have a spasm. There are better places to spend a night than a bellbuoy in a southerly off Cooper's Cove Reef.

When I was still below the shooting age, my father struck out one morning to go duck shooting with Cap'n Newcomb. He had asked a few special friends along, a dozen or so. They got aboard and headed out of the harbor in one of our fine fogs. You would get about the same effect by sticking your head in a paper bag. The world evaporates before you, and you are strangely alone. There is nothing to see, and if a chance spurt of wind parts the fog for an instant and you sight something, it never looks like what it is. Things begin to drip. Noises from beyond the periphery of your own hatbrim are muffled and enlarged, all at once, so nothing sounds the way it should. Seeing your hand before your face is almost impossible, but if you should see it, you won't be sure which hand it was. To strangers from beyond the coastal slope, such a fog is one of Nature's wonders. It is the fog you can cut with a knife. It is the pea-soup fog—but a rich, full, thick, sludgy pea soup well shot with peas and larded with salt pork. None of your watery pea soup. It is pea soup warmed up from three days ago, heavy with its own protein importance. It will float a horseshoe.

It is nothing for our boatmen to strike out in such a fog. They have compasses, most of them, but they also have a sixth, seventh, eighth and ninth sense of navigation which allows them to get around. Once the Nova Scotia passenger steamer anchored in a dead calm about ten miles outside our harbor to wait out such a fog, and before she'd been there half an hour about a dozen of our lobstermen had come up to look her over. They were out pulling their traps, and as they came by they noticed a variation in the customary echo of their engines, and they surmised something was there, so they swung about and went to see. The steamer was blowing her fog horn every few minutes, but that didn't mean anything, as all manner of vessels went by there blowing horns all the time. What puzzled them was why the echo should show a stationary obstruction. People on the steamer must have thought they were in a harbor, what with all the small boats popping around. So fog doesn't mean much, and it is sometimes a great help in duck shooting. You can sneak up in it, particularly when your boat is painted white like the Lallygag.

So Cap'n Newcomb went up into a narrow cove and anchored. He thought the fog would scale off and they'd have some shooting. And while they were all sitting there talking and waiting, they heard engine noise off to one side, and everybody jumped up and began to yell, and somebody began to work the lever on the fog horn while the engineer jerked the whistle cord. Another vessel was coming down on them out of the fog! Sound travels over water with astonishing fidelity, but when it has fog to penetrate too, the physical forces are both subdued and enhanced to such an extent that physicists have never quite explained it. A mere whisper will sometimes carry ten miles and sound like a bark of a dog. So people on farms along the shore heard this commotion with ease, and had no idea what was going on. The crew of the oncoming vessel heard it, too, and a collision was avoided. The stranger came along easily, and there was a ringing of bells, and then an anchor was dropped. It didn't go down very far, because the tide was going. It plopped in the mud a few feet under water, but the way it dropped anybody might have been plumbing the Sargasso Sea. It was the only place left in the cove with water enough to float the two vessels.

The new vessel was a United States Naval craft. Her deck was agog and aglow with men in uniform, and they lined up at the rail to look at the Lallygag and her men with shotguns. A petty officer stepped to the rail and called, "Where are we?"

Cap'n Newcomb appreciated his advantage. There will always be something in the down-east coastal native to make him superior to uniformed personnel. One of our commonest types of entertainment is to relate how an admiral asked advice of a clam digger. And to give us our due—the admiral was usually in trouble, and the clam digger usually helped him out of it. So Cap'n Newcomb pointed shoreward, as far as anybody could tell in that fog, and said, "The Simeon Goldthwaithe farm lays there." The conversation gradually thinned out after that until a coolness prevailed, and then a fairly decent animosity was engendered, and it was shortly thereafter that the petty officer threatened to use his influence, and Cap'n Newcomb told him to go ahead and use it—just as soon as he could find some place to go ashore. The real story is, and was, of course, that this naval vessel was lost. She was out on some kind of a trial, and the fellows on her didn't know where they were. By sheer accident they'd happened to put up into that cove, and by good luck they'd threaded the small channel without grounding.

It was at just this stage of the negotiations that the fog scaled off a little and revealed a few black ducks sitting in the water on the shoreward side of the Lallygag. The dozen hunters on board raced to the rail and opened fire, with Cap'n Newcomb blazing from his favorite perch in the pilot house. My father said the whole crew on the naval vessel took for cover, and ran up and down and back and forth, and there was a lot of shouting and giving orders, and somebody blew a bugle. In a moment, however, the United States Navy saw that it was not being attacked, but that the gentlemen on the Lallygag were just shooting a few ducks, and things subsided. After the ducks were retrieved, Cap'n Newcomb tooted his whistle, and my father and the other hunters all stood at attention and saluted, and somebody said, "Damn the torpedoes, full steam ahead!" and the Lallygag picked her way down the channel of the cove and out to sea. The navy followed, and they kept right at the sternwake for quite a while. Then they sighted a sparbuoy they recognized, and away they went off to the westward and out of the picture forever.

Times kept getting worse for Cap'n Newcomb. First, they put a law on spring hunting, and although he didn't pay any attention to it, it hurt his spirit. Hardly anybody went by boat any more. The railroad had finally won the mail contract, and we folks in the village got our mail when we were supposed to. Mother said it was nice to get an answer back before you'd forgotten what it was you wrote, or who you wrote to. Summer people began buying up the islands, and they began using small power boats. Some days Cap'n Newcomb would get steam up, sail out of the harbor, and then come right back in again and tie up. Instead of going three, he was now going two. The white paint faded, and the pine was showing through brown. Then came the day when Cap'n Newcomb "went one," except that he couldn't go at all alone, and he simply stayed at the wharf. The metal smokestack rusted out and blew off. The Lallygag was done except for Cap'n Newcomb's persistent attendance. The harbor master spoke of towing her out when the captain was "gone." When the captain was killed trying to help shingle the fire station, everybody said he shouldn't have been allowed up there. The once-nimble legs that had climbed rigging in all the oceans of the world had tightened up on the Lallygag, and he wasn't so spry in his eighties. Of course, everybody knew that once he had decided to help shingle, no power in town was big enough to keep him on the ground. It was his own neck to break. And he broke it. Nobody seemed too surprised.

They did tow the Lallygag off, and fixed her berth so the little power boats could come in on that side of the Town Landing. Summer people, not one of whom was worthy to have shaken old Cap'n Newcomb's hand, crowded on and off, and some of them the next "season" asked whatever became of the old character that "lived in the houseboat." My guess is that he and Cap'n Noah are in a thundering big ark, painted white, off yonder where the golden geese fly, and they're having an awful good time.

Saunders

THERE'S one thing our folks always did—whatever they wanted to do. The best example I know of it was Sophie Dorr, who rouged her cheeks. I say "rouged," although it was brighter red than any rouge I ever saw anywhere else. Women, in those days, didn't rouge their cheeks, or touch up their lips, the way they do now in my town. The first brazen hussy who tried that occasioned comment about the place that all over the world a paint job was the mark of a harlot. The old timers knew that from having been all over the world and having seen it, but it didn't make any difference—our girls did what they wanted to, too. So Sophie Dorr rouged her cheeks all her life, from the time she was a young girl and first came to town, and was the only painted creature around. Sophie, though, was never accused of improper conduct. It was a story of sorts.

Sophie was a "state girl." A ward of the state, she was

sent to board with the Wallace Pitman family, and helped keep house for her schooling. I've heard people tell how she looked as a child. Rawboned and angular, her pinched face always in a shawl or kerchief, and her bright red cheeks like the rising sun on a hazy July morning. Her background, before that, was never known. She didn't go to school long—the other children shunned her. But she stayed with the Pitmans always. Mother Pitman died, and the children grew up and moved on, and Sophie stayed to take care of old Wallace. Wallace was a butcher and kept to himself, and it didn't take Sophie all day to do his housekeeping, so she began working out. She never said much, and she'd work only for the captains' wives in the big houses. You had to have teakwood and mahogany and white oak in your house to have Sophie come and dust. She charged hardly anything—a few dimes in her hand would pay for the day's work. She was older when I first remember her. I used to be on my way to school, and along would come Sophie. She wore round skirts that came to the ground, and she walked with that gliding motion long skirts can give. She had her shawl up, and always carried an umbrella by the abdomen. Everybody spoke to Sophie—a most polite good-morning, and in return Sophie would say good-morning crisply in a rather sweet voice. Since then, of course, I've come to think of Sophie as a tremendous enigma, and I wish there were some way to ferret out the real story. Her dresses were at least a century old, and there must have been some place she got them. I never heard anybody opine that she made them, or even bought them. They did say that the Pitman family never had a woman who could wear Sophie's dresses, so it isn't likely they came from the attic. Anyway, she was a queer anachronism in our town, and the red cheeks were only part of it.

There was a story about the red cheeks. They said

Sophie had a birthmark, and it was a hideous red smear across one side of her face. To hide it, she colored the other side. It was a left-handed kind of camouflage, because Sophie with two cheeks was certainly more noticeable than Sophie would have been with one. Birthmarks weren't unknown, and we had stories about them without anybody's trying to hide them. We had a man with only one ear, and he used to tell how it was bit off by a policeman in Valparaiso, but we all knew it was a kind of birthmark. Then we had a widow woman over on the point who had a bunch of grapes on the back of her neck. It was a funny looking thing, but she made no effort to hide it, and we all knew it was a birthmark. So Sophie's birthmark came to be accepted in town for what it was, and if it was her whim to disguise it with red paint, it was Sophie's to do with what she listed. There did grow up an interest in just which side of her face was real, and which was colored. Nobody knew. Some of the women who had hired her had tried to tell by looking close, but Sophie's sharp eyes would look back at them, and they didn't persist.

Then, as things ran on, nobody really noticed Sophie any more. Wallace Pitman grew older and older, and Sophie took care of him and worked out. Her lanky figure, with the close-hauled shawl, stooped a little, until there came a day when Sophie was old, too. There was a little piece in the papers about Wallace Pitman being 100 years old, and Sophie had him all washed and carded for the photographers when they came to take his picture. Those who went in said the house was spotless—new paint everywhere, all washed and starched. And the photographers came away from the house and tried to find out around town about Sophie. She had stood in the background all the time, staring at them, her flaming red cheeks searing their memories for life.

Well, the thing went on a few more years. Wallace Pitman died, and Sophie inherited the house and furnishings. She worked out a while, and then didn't work out any more. Two or three of the old sea captain families made a point of keeping an eye on her—although all of her former employers, now, were gone. "Mother asked us to see that Sophie made out all right," one woman told me long afterward. And one bitter winter day somebody thought of Sophie and went to see if she was all right. They found her in bed, and the house cold. The Selectmen had her taken to the hospital, and they had to send up a snowplow to break a road for the ambulance. How long Sophie had been in bed they never learned. In the hospital she had as much care as the president of any railroad ever got. The Selectmen told the doctor he wasn't to spare any expense, and several of the old sea-faring families told him the same. The Wallace Pitman children telephoned by long distance to make sure Sophie was having good care. The whole town took a major interest in her condition, and it no doubt was a kind of proof that queer little Sophie had her place in town far beyond what anybody thought.

Then word went around that Sophie had died. The funeral was held the same day, and nobody in particular went to it. It didn't seem just right. Sophie hadn't ever encouraged people. They put her in the Pitman lot. Sophie had left a will, all made out properly. She left the house and furnishings to the town on condition that six rosebushes near the kitchen window be taken up "the following spring" and planted on her grave. You can see them there today, about the last of June—big red single-blown roses of the old hedge type, the kind that run wild and bloom and bloom no matter how little care they have. They have spread down the wall, and halfway across the back end of the burial ground, and you can smell them a hundred yards away. When they read the will at the Selectmen's office, Henry Pitcher said, "Them red cheeks is bound to go on and on, ain't they?"

That put the red cheeks in Henry's mind, so the next time he saw the nurse from the hospital, Henry said, "You'd know, Emmie, which one of Sophie Dorr's cheeks was the one with the birthmark?"

And Emmie said, "I don't suppose I have any right to tell you, but it's been on my mind, and I'm glad you asked. The truth is, Sophie didn't have any birthmark at all."

"Not on her cheek?"

"Not a sign. I washed her off, and her skin was as fair as a baby's, and it gave me the willies to see her laying on the pillow as white as the pillow was. She asked me the day she came conscious again if I'd washed her face clean, and I never thought and said I had."

Henry Pitcher said Emmie's eyes all filled up with tears, and she said, "Sophie just looked at me and said, 'You know, then.' I felt like a chicken-thief. Honest, it's been awful hard to keep from telling anybody. Sophie just made her face red because she liked red. I think people ought to know. There's too few of us would have guts enough to do a thing like that. I think it's better people know than not. It's kind of mixed up, somehow, but I think people should know."

It wasn't long before everybody knew. The older folks tried to figure up how long Sophie had been in town. It was at least 70 years that she painted her cheeks red. People tried to remember when the birthmark story first started. It was back beyond our memories. And the red roses are there yet to remind us of little Sophie Dorr, who never did very much else, but who went a lifetime doing the one thing she wanted to simply because she wanted to.

Nobody should discount the great educational value of the cow, and in my town almost every family had one or two. We had two most of the time, and when I was a dozen or so I was in full charge. They took considerable attention, and it might be that a youthful valet to two cows is prevented by his duties from engaging in deviltry about the community, or hanging around the pool halls. I also know that the educational advantages of having two cows sometimes prevented my prompt participation in school affairs.

This was a source of embarrassment to me. We had a yellow cow who wouldn't let down her milk. Modern dairy technicians explain with charts and tabulated summations that this is all a notion, and that no cow ever "held up" her milk. My advice to the dairy technicians is to go soak their heads, because this yellow cow could give or hold it at will, and it made my dairy program most irregular. My father and my uncle and several of the neighbors investigated my claim that the yellow cow held up her milk, and said I was right. One morning my mother came out to see, and she said the yellow cow held up her milk.

This yellow cow was gentle and kind, and she gave a sort of concentrated milk that was largely cream, and the fact that she held up her milk was no reason to discard her for something more amenable. We also had a big black cow who was reputed to have Hol-steen in her, and she never held up her milk. Her distended udder invited attention, and the merest stroke would send a stream like a faucet into the pail with a resounding twang that echoed among the timbers of the barn and made the rooster crow. The way roosters do when they hear something that might conceivably be interpreted as the crow of another rooster. This black cow didn't care one way or the other. It was all one to her. She would fill the pail up before you knew it, and there'd be a great foam on the top. Her milk wasn't so yellow and creamy as the yellow cow's, but there was more of it and she did not stint. It was a pleasure to milk her. But the time saved at the job was lost again when I sat down to coax the yellow cow. And many a morning, while I was coaxing, I would hear the last bell ring at the school a mile away, and I would still sit there and coax while I knew the morning exercises were progressing nicely, and sometimes until the second class was about to convene.

There was nothing I could do about it. The yellow cow would have her head stuck up and her eyes shut, and she'd be constraining every muscle she controlled, and her ears would be laid back like rushes before the storm, and she didn't care if school kept or not. We tried everything. We didn't know about playing music for the cows then, but I was advanced enough in my technique so that I sang sometimes. Lilting, gay, happy songs that should bring joyful coöperation to the heart of any yellow cow. But she lactated not. This would go on until the yellow cow got tired, and then she would relax with a kind of a snap, and I'd milk her. We tried giving her the grain first. We tried giving it to her afterward. We washed her apparatus with warm water. We rubbed her all over with a brush. We led her out for a drink. We exhausted the possibilities, but nothing worked. Some mornings she would pay no attention, and would give down her milk without a flicker, and then I would arrive at school before the bell rang and take my seat with the rest.

My mother, whom I love deeply, tried to explain this unfortunate difficulty to the principal. The principal was highly authenticated by the State Department, and had all manner of experience and perspicacity, but he didn't know anything about cows or my mother. After I had insinuated myself as unobtrusively as possible into the morning exercises for two or three mornings, I was called to his office to be confronted with the awful charge that I had been late every morning. This I acknowledged, and said that I had two cows to milk. The principal suggested it would be better if I arose earlier.

I'm afraid that principals never enjoyed their stay in our town. The salt air, the freshness of the clover meadows, the prevalence of gingery old sea captains, the utter satisfaction with things as they were contributed to all of us a certain armor against criticism from such as might have nothing better to do than teach school. I told him I got up as early as I saw any need of, and if he could think of some way to make the yellow cow give down her milk it would turn out to be a much better solution. I didn't use those words, but the idea was substantially as reported. He then wrote a note to my mother. I took it home and mother said she didn't think much of a man who wrote in that kind of a pipsy-wipsy woman's handwriting, and that was the extent of both the conversation and activity in that connection.

The next day I was late again, and the principal accused me of not delivering the note to my mother. I told my mother, and she sat down, and in her firm hand she splashed ink around for a few minutes, and gave me a note to take back. The note was polite and pertinent. It explained that I had two cows to milk in the morning, and that one of them was fractious by nature and refused to conform wholly to the time routine as established by the school committee, and that if it happened that I continued to be late, it was a matter wholly beyond any immediate control, and words to that effect. It was a clear, concise, and complete explanation of the matter, and the principal read it and sneered. The next morning he interrupted the reading of the psalm and called public attention to the arrival of "the late Mr. Gould."

Actually, the embarrassment wasn't too much. The scholars all tittered, but at least 75% of the boys knew what my yellow cow was up to and they were on my side, and I don't think the thing bothered me as much as the principal thought. One of the things growing boys ought to learn is when to quit. You should quit when you are ahead. The principal then began a demonstration of what happens to anybody when he fails to quit when he is ahead, and I have carried the lesson with me to this day. The principal then began to write letters to my parents, bickering over this business of being late. He pointed out that the thing was interrupting the entire opening program, and scholars refused to observe the need for promptness when one of their number constantly arrived after the business had commenced. Morale, he said, was being undermined. The influence was bad. This kept up quite a while, and my mother ignored the messages consecutively until she felt the thing had gone far enough.

The principal had written, "Isn't there something we can do to keep John from being late every morning?" Mother penned the following reply, "Don't start until he gets there."

An animosity between myself and the principal arose out of this matter, and it has continued unabated until this day. If I should meet him tomorrow on the street, I know that he would be embarrassed. The good feeling that I do not bestow on him, however, I have reserved to add to my love for my mother, and if anyone should ever try to tell her that I am not on her side, I think she would find it hard to believe.

The yellow cow, like all my various boyhood cows, ultimately passed to the butcher shop, and appeared the next week on the meat counters of town as heavy western beef. She never learned to give down her milk, and the patience, endurance, and fortitude I developed as I sat there on the stool stroking her bone-dry teats has gone with me always. I never loved her until I was grown up, and could look back and see that caring for her had contributed greatly to my development and character. This same thing, maybe, can be said for all the lessons I had in those days.

The mental processes of a cow are so different from those of a small boy that constant conflict prevails. When you want her to drink, she doesn't want to, but after you have led her back into the barn, she will blat for a drink. Nearly everything I could say about cows follows somewhat this pattern. We had one cow that had a blat on her that would make a freight train whistle gag. She was in magnificent voice most of the time, and as we weren't really rural folks, but had neighbors near enough so it mattered, I was instructed not to let this cow blat. Her blat was a perfect example of bending every effort. Her physical preparation began by getting down as low to the ground as she could, and then working up until every last inch of lung was pushed out between her vocal chords. The woods resounded. I have never known another cow who could do half as well. In hot weather her periodic desires for liquid refreshment were supposed to be answered with a pail of water before the community had time to swear out a warrant. Once a year this cow would have her maternal urges surge upon her, and she would then blat for fair. The first time this happened I didn't rightly know what ailed her, and toted pail after pail which she first refused to drink, and then tipped over. My father led her off up the road after supper, and when she came back she didn't blat again for a week. A year later, when motherhood beckoned again, I had things figured out, and I took her up to Deacon Bowles's myself, and was more or less comforted in my thirst for knowledge about what goes on in this old world of ours, anyway.

The blat on this cow teased me once into a one-boy attack on a minister I didn't like. This minister brought it on himself. He asked me why I didn't come to Wednesday night meetings, and I told him I went once. He replied that once was scarcely enough. I said once was more than I felt I needed, and he reported to my mother that I had sassed him on the street. This was news to me, and it took a day or so for me to figure out that our man-to-man conversation about the relative merits of meeting had been construed as sass. First, of course, I had denied any improper words, and this didn't work too well as rebuttal against the claims of the parson. But when I explained it to Mother she thought I had a point, and that was the end of the matter.

Not really the end, though, because I retaliated. When Sunday came around I neglected to administer any grain to my cow, and I failed to provide any water. I then led her to a point just at the rear of the church and tethered her with a short chain in a clump of dried up fern, alder shoots, and creeping myrtle. I then passed by on the other side and took my seat in church and gave my attention to devotions.

The cow did her best. She never did better. The pipes in the organ vibrated sympathetically. The minister didn't have a chance. Distortion must have set in as the ardent words of the prayer took flight for heaven. One of the deacons nudged me about the time of the thirdly and suggested I go and lead the cow to some distant place. I do not know if the deacon observed that after performing this errand I failed to return. A drink of water and a longer chain in a fine piece of sweet clover was my cow's reward, and my anger at the minister was allayed. I speak of this mostly to show that the onerous drudgery of a cow in your boyhood is not wholly a detriment, and that opportunity always stalks the alert and ready.

This cow ate too many August Sweets one afternoon, and they festered in her numerous stomachs and made her swell up. When I found her under the apple tree, whence she had strayed, her eyes were the length of peavey handles, her limbs were distended extensively, and her body was large and round. Her breath was not easy, and having heard the phrase from the older folks when they spoke of the departure of the sturdy pioneers, I observed that she was "dying hard." I raced for the house and reported that our cow was swollen up. They called the vet, who said he would come at once, and he did along in the middle of the afternoon in a badly intoxicated condition and a buffalo fur coat. The intoxication wasn't unusual, and to those who may remember our vet, neither was the coat. In the meantime, however, our cow had rallied after a home-spun treatment from the man across the street.

The man across the street was another of our world travelers who had settled down after a lifetime abroad and around about, and he knew all things. He came with an ice pick and punched a hole in my cow, and she subsided like a punctured football, and inside of five minutes she was eating again and looked all right. The man said the cowboys out west all had punches on their jackknives, so they could let the air out of cows that bloated, and it wasn't anything serious at all. When the vet came he fell over the tie-out chain and walked around the cow, and said she had "impaction of rumen" and had recovered and would be all right. This cost us two dollars, and at least one of the things I learned was that a cow shouldn't eat too many apples. There was a time in my life that I thought anybody with a fur coat and a quart of whiskey could practice as a veterinarian, but I also learned that sick animals are more often cured by the owner's care. A pail of warm water at the right time will do more for a sick cow than a vet, and of course faithful feeding and grooming all along will keep most cows from ever being sick at all. I have never punched a cow, but there was a time I was sure I'd try it if the August Sweets ever swelled one up again.

I haven't mentioned the greatest benefit that comes to the growing boy who keeps a cow. It is the tall glass of cold milk on the table, and plenty of cream for the morning oatmeal, and the big bowl of butter that nobody ever bothered to press in pound patterns. There were big jorums of ice cream that would astonish the ice cream people today—they were made with milk and eggs and had fruits in them. Millionaires can't buy that kind of boyhood, but any lad could have it by taking care of a cow. I hate to dwell on these advantages, because they make me hungry, and a little weepy. I am glad I had a cow in my boyhood. They made me late for school, but I guess I didn't miss much.

N O BOY ever grew up right unless he learned to fish. Our fishing was two kinds—we had the whole great Atlantic Ocean, and we had the small brooks that came down off the hills. Boys didn't get to fish the ponds and lakes of inland Maine so much—there was a curious belief on the part of the mothers that while George's Banks were all right, fresh water was dangerous. We did, once in a while, find a chance to sneak off for salmon, perch and bass. Perch and bass we caught, always, by mistake—that being sound Maine attitude. I don't know why that is, but even today a true Maine sportsman looks upon perch and bass as a handliner looks at dogfish and skate. Trout is your real Maine inland fish.

My boyhood was in the fish-pole era. They are rods today. My father took me fishing for the first time when I was five, and he says I caught a brook trout that weighed an even pound. I snaked him from behind a log, and my father says he had to chase me down—I started for home dragging the fish, and Father was afraid I'd wear it out. But my real fishing tutor was Bill Damon. Bill was queer, and every once in a while he would beat up his wife, and throw all the furniture in the street, and break a lot of windows, and punch a lot of men in the nose when they came to take him away. They would take him away for a while, but then he would come home and be all right. And while he was all right, he would take us boys fishing. Bill caught fish when there weren't any fish, and he was a big factor in truancy. On the way to school on a good spring morning, Bill would meet us, and he'd say, "If you was to have your druthers, which would you druther—go fishing?" This was an invitation, and we all of us would certainly druther, but Bill never took but one boy at a time. I've often wished there was a good answer to Bill's query. We had a lot of similar queries, but most of them had an answer. A favorite was, "Do you think they'll have it?" Strangers look perplexed at that and usually say, "Have what?" But anybody who grew up in my town knew the right answer. I suspect it came from the days of wagon circuses, because the proper answer is, "The tents are up!" I'd like to have a nickel for every time I've engaged in that illuminating byplay. Of course, it was merely a manner of greeting, and wasn't supposed to mean anything.

Going fishing with Bill was so common an event that once in school the teacher asked if anybody knew why Robert Sawyer wasn't present, and without thinking I said, "He went fishing with Bill Damon." Bob never took me to account for it, and the teacher never mentioned it again. The truth is that going fishing with Bill was better learning than the schools gave us, although perhaps the teacher didn't realize that at the time. Bill never let the catching of fish become the prime purpose of the expedition. There were caddis eggs to see, and skunk cabbages coming through the moss. Bill pointed them all out. He knew what trout were eating, and showed us how to fix the bait. Along later he shifted to flies, and showed us how to tie them. He had a way of laying a trout on coals and making it taste so you wouldn't believe it, and when he felt like carrying a knapsack, he had a way of making a trout chowder so a whole pail full was scarcely enough for both of us. Then Bill would beat up his wife again, and punch out some more windows, and we wouldn't see him for a while.

Salt water fishing was rarely thought of as sport. Fresh water fishing would have been wholly sport, except for the pleased look on Mother's face when she saw a mess of trout coming home on an alder crotch. One time we had company, and some of us went up the brook, and we caught trout enough to feed 17 people. Mother stood at the stove and fried them, and we ate them as fast as they came out of the pan until nobody could get up from the table. Mother asked if she should wash the pan afterward, or just throw it away, and everybody laughed. It was an enormous mess of trout, one of the biggest I've ever seen.

In those days the rivers and streams of Maine hadn't suffered from pollution, and the forests hadn't been cut back to the quick so the streams warmed up. We got our sea-run trout then, and the big ones that would come up from the ocean to spawn. The sea-run trout and our Eastern Brook Trout are the same thing, and they are the only true trout. The Rainbow, and the Dolly Varden, and the Loch Leven make pretty names, but there isn't a trout any better than our cold- and quick-water speckled trout. There isn't one so good, even. They'd come up from the brackish tidewater after the glass eels, and gradually work up the streams until a can of worms would produce some amazing results. We'd still have these trout today if the water was fit for them to come into, but the politicians seem to be much more interested in how big a hatchery they can build, and I gather the number of trout you can plant in a stream has some bearing on the vote every two years. The difference is further illustrated by the change from "fish-pole" to "rod." We cut an alder pole with our jackknives every time we went. The brooks were lined with alder, and nobody cared how much alder we cut. And in our pockets we always had the gear that sportsmen now refer to as tackle. Ours was a piece of ganging—pronounced gainjing. It is a coarse cord, used for codlines and potheads, and modern anglers would claim it couldn't possibly take a trout. Our hook was a common cunner hook—a cunner being a salt water fish that has a sweet, nutlike meat and makes nice chowders. The hooks were always set into a cork stopper, so they wouldn't foul our pockets, and if we wanted a bob for still-water fishing, we had the cork. Every boy in my town carried in his pocket at all times something in the way of a nail, in addition to his knife, his ganging, and whatever else he needed, and the nail could quickly become a sinker if a sinker was thought useful. The entire outfit represented an outlay of about three cents, and since my youth I have seen excited sportsmen lay down a hundred dollars at a crack for trout equipment, and wonder if they had enough to get by. Today, and I'm far from a boy now, I still carry a hank of twine and a nail, and find a dozen uses for both every week. If I pick up a hook, I'm ready to go trouting again, and I find Bill Damon knew as much as anybody needs to know about lures and methods.

There are only two ways to cook a trout of brook size. He should be mulled in deep pork or bacon fat, previous to which it is proper to roll him in white flour, corn meal, or cracker crumbs. Most people singe him on the bottom of a hot pan, and are much too sparing with the fat. The other way is to make a chowder, and you need a generous catch. A trout chowder is as simple as any fish chowder, starting with salt pork on the bottom of the kettle and working up to a slow and lingering simmer so people a mile away will have plenty of time to smell it and envy you until their hair has turned green. Bill Damon taught us to steam the trouts until we could pick the meat off the bones, and pick the black skin off the meat. Then you add the meat to the pork and potatoes and onion and milk and seasoning, and recline against a convenient stump and smell it until you can't stand it any longer. As far as I know, there are no other ways to cook trout. Somehow, none of the other fish we caught as boys comes through to me now—the bass and pickerel and perch never registered.

Hornpout, Maine's only member of the catfish family, were taken best after dark, and we didn't get to go for them much. They are a nice fish, and tasty, and almost impossible to kill. You can leave them sitting in the hot sun in a pail for days, and they will jump out at you. They are not good Maine. The chubs and shiners, dignified by poor Isaac Walton as Chavender and known in some places as dace, we ignored—unless we were thoughtful enough to bring one home to the cat. We did go and spear suckers in the spring, but I've always wondered why. Everybody always said the sucker was nice eating if you took him in the spring from cold water, but I never knew of anybody who ate one. I learned in later years that suckers are known in New York as Mountain Trout, which is probably all right. I would recognize him as a sucker, I think. I planted some corn on suckers once, the way the Indians used to, but the 'coons came and dug up the suckers and the enterprise was not a success. After they dug them up, the 'coons wouldn't eat them, and I have had great respect for the intelligence of 'coons ever since. The puckered-up mouth of a sucker shows how he feeds off the bottom, and as a gamefish he has about the same ferocious nature as a cucumber. I would rather have trout. A trout will smash at your bait like a freight engine, and will be off down stream before you know he is around, and I have never brought one to the bank without admiring his agility. I have never eaten one without congratulating myself.

I prefer to fish a brook. Bill showed me so many interesting things to look for, that a brook without trout is still a treat. I like to haggle with the early trout, when the water is almost running ice, and I have to wait and wait and wait for him to get the bait in his mouth. And I rather enjoy flipping a fly on the water in later summer, and seeing that splash of speckled color explode in my face. I like trout best, though, when he is fried in deep pork fat. And I've never started off without hearing, somewhere in the background, Bill Damon's little greeting, "Which would you druther, go fishing?" Indeed I would.

NOT long ago I practically undermined the Boy Scout movement. When I was a boy in my town, the Boy Scouts were not yet prevalent, and I'm afraid I never felt the lack as keenly as a boy might today. Our closeness to nature gave us information and knowledge that Boy Scouts will never get, and we probably benefited from the unsupervised manner in which we mastered the subjects. Anyway, not long ago a real Boy Scout happened to say he was having a little difficulty with his knots. He had a piece of sashcord which he had almost worn out, and for some reason the knots simply wouldn't come. I found out, as I frequently do when I plumb modern learning, that the boy didn't realize that knots are tied for a purpose. His scoutmaster had given him the cord, and had shown him how to use it, but the scoutmaster had failed to make it plain that a knot is intended to assist in a utilitarian purpose. I couldn't teach the boy his knots either, until I found out that all he needed was something to tie. I showed him how easy it is to keep a cow to a fencepost with a clove hitch—and after that he learned knots without any trouble.

One of the knots he had trouble with was a reef knot, and he didn't understand how it could possibly be used for anything. He didn't call it a reef knot, but I knew what he meant. He called it a square knot. So I dropped back to my own generation, and went through the same routine that the old ship masters had used with me. I told him a square knot was the proper knot for reefing sails, and I explained how that was done and why it was done, and I said, "The beauty of it is in the speed with which you can untie it." I gave the knot a jerk, slipped it by, and there was the sashcord untied. So the boy practiced it, and he saw how it was, and then he worked on the bowline a while, and a few nights later he went to his Boy Scout meeting and showed the scoutmaster how to untie a reef knot. The scoutmaster insisted something was wrong. He insisted a square knot couldn't be untied that easy, and came to the belief that he was making a mistake in what he was teaching the boys. A square knot, according to him, was a secure and trusty knot, and he felt anything that came apart in his hands must be tied wrong. So he told the boy that was not a square knot, and it couldn't be a square knot so long as it came untied so simply. I dropped the subject after that, because I knew in this day and age nobody would appreciate remarks about the masthands who stood on the footropes and jerked the great sails free according as commands came from the deck below. A square knot, in this generation, must stay tied, and I leave it there.

Cap'n Ethan Starbird taught me knots. He'd stick his wooden leg up on a chair, and I'd bend all manner of knots and hitches around it. Each knot had its purpose. It did a certain thing. All the important knots, those a man on shore is likely to need in his lifetime, came first. Then he showed me those intricate things that sailors thought up to show how smart they are. He showed me how to tie off the end of a rope, and then he showed me how to serve it if it was to pass through a block. He taught me the long splice and the short splice, and we used up rope enough to rig a schooner. Only he never called it rope, because on board a vessel they don't have many ropes. They tell about "learning the ropes" but it doesn't take long to learn the ropes. The lines and sheets and halyards and warps are the hard ones. They use a rope to pull the clapper in the ship's bell, and they use a rope to hang onto in a storm, and maybe two or three others—but in my town hardly anybody ever spoke of a rope. Cap'n Ethan would sometimes end up a knot lesson with his wooden leg displaying more knots than the Boy Scouts ever heard of.

There is a lot to know about rope, too, besides how to tie it. Cap'n Ethan explained how slack rope can be taken up by wetting it—a pail of water will bind any load on a cart, and if you're towing something across the bay you want to leave slack where it can be found when you come to unbind. And about buying rope. In our town rope was sold in the stores in two ways—they kept it in the damp cellar and sold it by the pound, or they kept it in the hot attic and sold it by the foot. Rope-wary old sea-dogs knew these tricks, and the storekeepers gave them a choice. Cap'n Ethan, when he had to buy line, would watch his barometer, and if he bought by the pound on a dry air, he'd get six or eight feet more rope for the same price.

But the point was, I suppose, that as a boy I was told or shown what each knot was used for. There was a way to make a hitch on a cask, there was a knot for lowering a painter over the side of a vessel. There were knots for a

killick that wouldn't come unfastened, and there were
knots that would jerk free in an instant. There was a way
to tie on a codhook, and a way to fasten a skiff to a moor-
ing buoy. It was all there, and once we knew what the
idea was, we had no difficulty at all with the knots. And
after Cap'n Ethan had done his best, there was still more
to learn. My mother showed me a weaver's knot because
that was one Cap'n Ethan never heard of and she knew I'd
show him and make him chuckle. And my uncle recalled
his days in the West, and showed me how to hogtie a crit-
tur. I showed them to Cap'n Ethan, of course, and while
he adopted the weaver's knot as useful and "a mite tricky,"
he said the hogtie idea was a highlander's makeshift, and
besides it was illegal in Maine. Almost anything is illegal
in Maine when you come right down to it, and he probably was right.

Cap'n Ethan told me once that the idea of a model
ship was ridiculous. He made them, and made them well,
but he said the trouble with model makers was that they
rigged their models right. A vessel, in the old sailing days
of New England, was rigged right only when she was new.
Inside of fifteen minutes the Yankee crew had broken
something, and like all Yankees anywhere, they had immediately fixed it. Sometimes they improved on it, and
sometimes they didn't, but whatever they did, it was fixed
different when they got through. Cap'n Ethan said he had
seen every kind of combination of masts, spars and rigging
that the mind of man could invent or the hand of man
could devise, and most of them would all be on one vessel
before she got back from her first voyage. So, an accurate
model of the Ship Ovation would be completely incorrect
if she was rigged the way a ship should be rigged, because
the Ovation was never rigged that way that anybody could
remember. And Cap'n Ethan said neither was any other
Maine vessel that he ever saw. Every one of the old skip-

pers in my town tried making a model one time or another, and I soon noticed that when they showed her, they always said something like, ". . . rigged as she was in '54." It helps explain, maybe, the skill with ropes that came to us boys, because from the earliest time we had drilled into us the important information that a rope was not a thing by itself, but was devised for useful chores.

Another thing that went with ropes were the definitions of things aboard ship. Cap'n Ethan made me memorize the names of the masts and the names of the sails. He told me once about the famous Thomas W. Lawson, the only seven-masted schooner ever built, and how they had trouble naming her aftermast. In working a vessel, which was quite a job on the bigger schooners and windjammers, the name of the mast was important, because orders from below had to be carried out quickly, and if a man was up the wrong mast and pulled the right rope, he might make himself appear silly at times. The three masts on a ship were the fore, main and mizzen. And a ship, incidentally, was never anything in my day but a three masted vessel rigged under plain sail, or topsail rigged. The Queen Mary may be so called, but she is never a ship to me. Brigs, barques, barquantines, "Morphodites," schooners, and all such derived differences in their masts and rigging, and none of them was a ship. The fourth mast became a spanker, and then the jigger and driver masts. When the Lawson went into construction, she was a steel vessel, a compromise came up, and there were those who tried to work her with the days of the week. The Sunday mast was the foremast, etc., and that left Saturday for the seventh, un-named, mast. But there were those who used the word pusher mast, and among my people it stuck. Great arguments have arisen over the names of the masts on the Lawson, but Cap'n Ethan told me, and I know. Once in Boston a smart man chided me about growing up in a small shipping town, and because he owned a yawl out at Marblehead he thought he would show off, and he said he bet me I didn't know the names of the masts. Cap'n Ethan told me once, "These things I tell you, someday you'll find there's pleasure in the knowing." So I rattled off the seven masts, and started up the mainmast with the sails, and the smart man in Boston happened to think of something important he meant to do, and left me in my pleasure. The next time I was in my town I intended to tell Cap'n Ethan about it, but the dear old pirate had wrapped the sailcloth about him and laid down to pleasant dreams of his own.

Cap'n Ethan had another good story about the two six-masted schooners. There were only two afloat, and old mariners would go to the wharves when they were in and gaze upon them. Under full sail they were something to see, and their speed was duly discussed on all the back porches of our town at the time. They represented a terrific investment, and were a far cry from the small vessels our men had built on the front lawns a generation or two before. So these two six-masted schooners were afloat, and they were the only two six-masted schooners on the seas. And one night in Boston harbor they collided. I forget the details, but they could be looked up. The important thing to remember was the completely impossible coincidence of the thing. It was fantastically unlikely, but there it was. And Cap'n Ethan used to say, "But it was like that all the time—we'd stop at a little island in the Indian ocean for water, and go ashore, and there would be somebody from Poppycock Hill hanging out his wash on a wild cucumber vine, and we didn't think anything of it." Coincidence, I think, is an important factor in human life, and sometimes vexes untutored people, but we boys learned about it, and have been seldom surprised.

Cap'n Ethan's stories were inexhaustible, and as long

8▶155

as I practiced my splice, or worked on a Blackwall hitch for his wooden leg, he would talk and talk, and I learned and learned. "I raced the whole British navy once," he started off. The British navy, like the American navy, always comes out second best with our merchant mariners in Maine, and while some evidence might be assembled to prove the Maine men are stretching the warp, I doubt if it would be either reliable or enjoyable. "I raced them for a cask of rum, and I won."

If he hadn't won, I would not have heard the story—I was old enough to know that. There is a trick to listening to these old yarns, and perhaps the age of telling might have lasted longer if we had bred better listeners. We boys knew how to listen. "Is that right?" I'd say. And I wasn't questioning his preface to a story. I was ignoring the story. I was asking about the knot I was doing. Cap'n Ethan would lean over and gaze at his leg. "Pass through the bight from under . . ." he'd say, and I would pass up through and draw tight so his wooden leg would hop up off the chair.

"Liverpool was a great place for racing. Every time we'd get there somebody would want to race us. They had a great respect for our Maine lumber, and they knew we fashioned it right. The English are great sports, but they never learned to size up their chances. They'd take on anything, and sometimes it wasn't too smart a thing to do, but they'd do it, and if they took a trimming, they'd pay up without a squawk and shake hands and almost seem to apologize for putting you to the trouble of beating them. Used to be a great ambition of everybody with a fleet vessel to get to Liverpool with her and win a race before the rigging got rimracked. We'd try a new vessel out, and then think up excuses to get to Liverpool. Shift the free end to your left hand."

"Like that?"

"No, pass it under your thumb, so—now, make the turn . . ."

The wooden leg would hop up again.

"We had a little speed we didn't know where we got in the Joyce Ann, and I thought we might have some fun. So on the run before the wind into British waters we went amongst the whole British navy and we saluted and tooted and felt pretty cocky, and one of them spoke us and challenged us to a race for a keg of rum. I blatted back that they were on, and we run up everything to the dishrag and struck out. Well, every cussed ship they had afloat come about at the same time, and they all took down wind with us like a convoy. They had sloops and corvettes and brigs and everything both up and down, and the men stood in the rigging and cheered, and we cheered back, and it looked like the milltail of a hurricane in a sheet factory, and there we were all hightailing along to glory and we didn't have the faintest idea which vessel it was we were racing. They got all mixed up. There was a little sloop come up under our looward and the sailors on her all grinning like the breech in a busted barn, and I thought she was going to go by, but she swamped and went under, and whilst she went those sailors stood right there grinning and cheering, and the rest of us kept right on going and nobody so much as looked back. That's the way we used to race into Liverpool. You got it there, now —do that one again, and don't draw it quite so tight, it's supposed to be slack.

"So we thundered along in, and we beat 'em. We were away out front, and then we come closer to the shore-line and we had to taper off, and we went on into the harbor. Well, come evening a lighter drew up alongside us, and a sailor come aboard with his pants legs flapping, and he saluted so his backbone twanged like a banjo, and he said, 'His excellency, Sir Lord So-and-so, Keeper of the

Privy and Knight Comma-w-nder of the Bawth, presents his compliments and wishes to discharge the obligations of his wager,' or something about as fancy as that, and we went and looked, and there on the lighter was 42 casks of Jamaican rum. It was quite a haul, and I returned his compliments and awsked his excellency to come over and have a drink, but he never come. I didn't know we had been racing the whole fleet. For years I shuddered in my sleep every time I'd dream about how expensive it would have been to lose, and I guess sometimes it's a good thing not to know what you're up against."

No doubt the older folks of the town had heard that story so often that Cap'n Ethan was telling it to me as a last resort. In fact, some of the stories I heard were in the public domain, and each skipper told them as if he were the hero. There was a favorite about the skipper from Belfast who had himself coopered in an empty barrel so he could be smuggled aboard his ship past the police in Rangoon, and because the sailors didn't like him they jounced him around considerable with the hoist, and when they got to sea and let him out, they found he'd broken his leg somehow. I suppose every Maine mariner who ever had so much as one toe in the water was an accredited and bona fide member of that crew, and had personally knocked the head off the barrel. But that doesn't matter, the important thing is that the story was so, and was a good story, and it got told to boys like me who had receptive ears and a lifetime in which to assess it.

But when the Boy Scout came and asked me to show him his knots, I felt extremely inadequate. I wish I might have been Cap'n Ethan with a wooden leg and a story. The Boy Scout movement is a fine thing, and I don't belittle it at all—I simply can't help thinking we'd need it less if we had more Cap'n Ethans. And Bill Damons, and others of the kind that helped me grow up.

E<small>VEN</small> today, in an age known as enlightened, Maine
has a law forbidding drinking in public places. This, to
the thoughful, would indicate that private drinking is lawful, which is probably so, but it also gives discerning
police officers the chance to decide as occasion demands
how many people it takes to make a place public. At
times exceedingly different interpretations have been
made, and while two cow jockeys behind a barn have been
considered close to a violation, great throngs attended by
a number of public officials have appeared to be very
private, indeed. But Maine was always like that. Most of
her citizens have always been temperate, and even abste-
mious, on the grounds that liquor is an expensive habit
and should not be expected to lead to anything but cha-
grin. The state has, however, been notoriously promis-
cuous in its adaptability to whatever could be poured out
the soonest, and intoxication has been noticeable right

along—even if you make allowances for the fact that one drunk can be as ubiquitous as all outdoors.

Our town had a Town Drunk. I'm afraid he was not too good an object lesson for temperance instruction—but that was like our town, and even our town drunk had his instructive capacity for, I'm afraid, great good if you could but grow up there and drink deep of his clear-running tide. The metaphor may be confused, but even that is a part of this story. Because Leslie Burbage was a great man, and his addiction to alcoholism seemed to play no part at all in his career—aside from the fact that he was drunk a good part of the time and none of the old ladies could figure out where he got the stuff. In fact, Les was the sort of successful man little boys might be expected to hold as a hero, with the intention of growing up to be like him. The fact that none of us (that I know of) did is a tribute, maybe, to the evenness of our times, and the great discernment and perspicacity that came to us to spare us any such a thing. I'm not sure I can exactly show how Les played his part in the scheme of life we grew up into—but at least I can tell about him with honest chronicling, and show that he had his place. It might be easier if he hadn't been a drunk.

We had other drunks, one of whom was Judge Proctor, but as I think back not one of them seems to come up wholly to the "no good end" standards, and they must have all been hopeless disappointments to the little ladies with the white ribbons who met every week and discussed the evils of drink. Judge Proctor kind of complicated our local attitude toward the bibulating offender, because it was perfectly clear from the beginning that nobody was likely to win punishment from him on any such charge as intoxication. Stealing lobsters, or lighting fires in barns, or failure to pay bills had at least an equal chance before him, but intoxication was a mental condition, he said, and should not be dealt with in the unsympathetic halls of statutory justice. The temperance movement, aside from social and political complications, was licked from the start through the chance fact that our judge liked a snort himself, and was not above admitting it from the bench. So the town had long since abandoned any hope of reforming Les Burbage through any writ or summons, and if the constabulary stepped in, which was seldom necessary, all they did was take Les home and put him to bed.

Sometimes Judge Proctor did mete out ten days in the county jail to new offenders, or strangers, and if mitigating circumstances urged it, the ten days were readily probated and the fine suspended. The costs were suspended, too. Besides, the dusty old law office where Judge Proctor held court would resound with a stirring address by the presiding justice on the nature of society's obligations to the wayward and weak. He said the laws about intoxication were made by nincompoops who didn't know whiskey from a pot of cold tobacco juice, and he had never heard of an authenticated instance where jail had reformed a drunkard. He would then charge the arresting officer to use more discretion in the future, and say that things had come to a pretty pass when an upright, honest, hard-working, sober citizen couldn't take one stinking little drink without getting hauled up for it. You can see what I mean when I say our temperance instruction was confused.

At the same time, let me affirm, we were to all appearances a prohibition people in a prohibition town in a prohibition state, and we were constantly reminded that wine is a mocker and strong drink is raging, and that he who would thrive and prosper should find merit in Adam's Ale and stick to it. We had regular instruction in school on Frances E. Willard day, and Mrs. Conrad M. Mountfort would come and show us that an angleworm, dropped into a glass of whiskey, would die. We wondered where she got the whiskey, but it was considered impolite to probe these side-issues of education. I found out later that anybody, dropped into whiskey, will die. The result of this variety of conflicting instruction was to bring up a generation that differed little from the one before, and I understand while the town is dry today by local option, and temperance instruction is still presented, an occasional drunk arises to perplex the thoughtful, and to temper the learning of little boys.

Les Burbage was a large man, who would weigh about 200 without an ounce of excess flesh on his generous frame. He could fell an ox with a blow of his fist, which is a manner of speaking because I never knew of anybody to do it, but he was gentle and tender, and was never known to exhibit his strength for sheer show. He was usually in farm clothes, but had dress-up ones for high school functions, or Town Meeting, or Grange times. When he was shaved his face was pinky and pretty, and showed a youthfulness for all his sixty or so years of failure to take care of himself as the saying runs. He never had a toothbrush in his mouth, and he had every tooth he ever had as sound as a nut. It certainly was confusing.

A kind of alarm ran about town when he got drunk again. People passed the news one to another, the ladies sighed at his weakness, and then men wondered what would happen now. Something always happened. But never to Les. Les had a charmed life, and things would break loose in his vicinity and lay things waste, but Les would get up and stagger home untouched. One day in Howdy Baston's blacksmith shop Les had leaned back against the barrel of water used for tempering metal, and had gone to sleep. His legs were spread on the floor, and he was dead to the world. Howdy was trying to put a shoe on a green horse that somebody had brought in from the west. He had a line to her hind leg, holding it up, and a twister on her nose so she was holding her head up against the rafter and blowing like a porpoise with asthma. Jim Treach was holding the twister, and he was good at it, and all at once the horse decided the whole thing was an awful waste of time, and the program should be terminated. Howdy and Jim and the six or eight other men around put for the door and rolled it shut, leaving Les propped there against the barrel. The horse raced around inside the shop for ten or fifteen minutes, knocking everything down that was standing up, and standing up everything that was down, and Les kept on sleeping. Then the horse tried to jump through a six-by-nine light of glass in the rolling door, and took down the whole front end of the shop, and proceeded in a westerly direction for quite some distance. The men came back in, and Les was still asleep.

He had tough luck with one team he owned when I was a boy. They were heavy, and paired beautifully. They stepped off together with their heads up, and could do delicate work in the woods without reins on them, just by Les's speaking to them and sucking through his tooth. One night he had them up to the village, and a blizzard shut down. Les was feeling good, in fact he was roaring drunk and had been going from store to store comparing prices and swearing at each storekeeper because he was charging more than another for something. And he piled onto the front bunk of his logging sleds, unwound the reins from the stake, and started off for home just as the storm was settling into something mean. He was hanging onto the sled stake and making a lot of talk, and off he went. Well, he got to the railroad tracks, and the night train went by just at that time and snaked his team of horses right out of the harnesses, and spread them out for a considerable distance up the track. Nobody in the train knew anything about it, and neither did Les. He sat there in the snow, yelling, and stayed sitting there all night. Four other trains went by before morning, and then they found Les sitting there with snow very much in evidence. If he'd been sober, he'd have died, they said. Froze to death. But he was all right, and they took him home in a sleigh and dug his sleds out, and went up and down the track looking for parts of the horses, some of which they found. Les said he didn't hear any whistle, and it was probably so.

But there was something about this that didn't seem to jibe with admonishments. Les was very much alive, when we knew not another man in town would have survived. The split-second saving of his life through the mysterious division of his passage into foot-by-foot degrees of danger was a phenomenon reason couldn't probe. Nothing happened to Les, ever. Once his horses ran away and took him and his mowing machine across country, but he came back uninjured. He was mowing, and they said a moose blew in the bushes near by. Horses will run from moose, and Les's horses did. They ran about five miles, going over stone walls and through the woods, across a couple of brooks, and wreaking fearful damage as long as the cutter bar continued to work. It brought up on something at last, and was bent around so it sort of laid out back and snapped at Les every time it bounced. Les came back by way of the Poppycock Hill road, and about all he had left of his machine was the pole, wheels, and seat. But he didn't have a scratch on him, and he'd mowed down a lot that never was mowed before or since.

He officiated generously at burning buildings. Whenever a fire blew in, Les would charge into the house and begin moving out furniture. He'd keep at it until he usually came out a burning brand himself, and the hose crew always stood ready to put him out. Many a time I've seen him spinning off across a field with a stream on him, and he'd plow flat on his face for ten feet—but he never got burned or hurt. He used to go jigging mackerel, and he usually tipped over. Word would run around about who picked him up this time and towed his boat in. He fell in the hopper at the grain mill once, making quite a yell while he went, and they shut the machinery down just as the grinders took his bootheels off. At the sawmill he was ramming around once, and he got his coat caught on the carriage and went whining down to glory along with a log. He went by the saw so close that when the board came off he was free on the other end, and he stepped down. It never touched him. Chin Garland, the sawyer, had a fainting spell on account of it, and had to shut the mill down and sit still for most of the afternoon. And Les had fallen off beams, into wells, out of trees, off wharves, and all such things as that so many times nobody could remember—and he had never been to a doctor or had a doctor come to see him.

This isn't the whole catalog of close calls by any means. Les never let a suitable day pass without doing his part to refute the claims that alcohol brought on grief and misery. There was, instead, a solemn belief that if Les had lived a sober minute, he'd have died instantly. Les never gave this theory a chance, and continued to pursue the habit to the end. Furthermore, Les led a perfectly harmonious life at home, and was a prosperous and forward-looking farmer. He had the best fields and animals in town. His house was painted, his lawn was mowed, his flowers were gorgeous. His wife was perhaps the prettiest woman in town, right up to the time age changed her face. She was a Campbell from Harpswell, and was noted in her 'teens as the prettiest thing Harpswell ever bred. Which is saying a good deal, too. She never let on in any way that liquor had soiled her life, and there was never the faintest suggestion that she thought Les was any different from anybody else. Mrs. Burbage had things in her house that other women envied, and she wore nice clothes and went anywhere she wanted to go. The children were as smart as steel traps, and always led their classes in school. I can remember the lunch buckets they brought with them. The drunkard's children ate well. They had jars of preserves that used to scent the whole room with all the odors of summertime when they'd open them, and mere sandwiches were never included in the dinners. They brought cold cuts of meat, and slices of homemade bread spread with great gobs of yellow butter, and big pickles that made our mouths pucker to look at them, and whole pies that they'd cut up and eat with forks.

None of us, in those days, shared the present-day horror of cold lunches. I wish the people who larrup around over hot lunches today could have seen our dinner-time spreads at school. We children ate like hired men at noon, and had things a hired man would need. Our lunches were called dinners, and they were prodigious. And good. My mother was as good as any mother about this, and I fancy she would smile at hot lunches if anybody asked her. Good for the under-privileged, maybe, but I don't remember that anybody was under-privileged then, if lunches were anything to go by. The worst I can recall from my school days was the sad case of Stuart Millikin, who never had more than a biscuit and an apple for noon—but that was because he ate his dinner at recess. He got hungry and couldn't wait. A hot lunch might have been a great help to him. The rest of us didn't need it, we had all we could do to eat the cold ones—and I will swap the gourmet's finest banquet right now for what Holman Day called "the infinite gusto from the depths of the old dinner pail." Noontime was hard work, the way we ate, and Les Burbage's children ate as hard as any of us. When we could swap a piece of raspberry pie with a Burbage for a filled cookie, we thought we made a good trade. And in fact, we did, which is no slam at our own mothers, but is praise for Mrs. Burbage.

Les would dress up for any function where his children were taking part. They loved their father. He always held them on his knees riding in a pung or buggy, and would hold hands walking. When he'd come to school speaking contests or sociables, he'd get all dreamy eyed and weepy while he watched Doris, who looked like her mother, parade around in seven-in-and-seven-out, or Teddy stand up and speak. So the thing went, and if anybody had looked into the thing, I imagine Les would have come up with some interesting remarks that might be construed as philosophy. But he remained our Town Drunk right through to the end, and seemed to baffle the folks who hoped he would go down to perdition so they could say, "I told you so." Les didn't. He died a few years back at 87, going on 88, and he was hale and hearty, and drunk, right up to the last. He got the measles. He'd never had any children's ailments, and the measles took him off over night. The best the hopefuls could get out of that was to say he'd have lived longer if he hadn't undermined his resistance with drink. I don't believe it, myself, because at 87, going on 88, a man has a right of his own to die anyway he pleases, and I don't think sobriety needs to be a factor, pro or con.

It was true, though, that our town had other drunks who didn't muddle the temperance lessons quite so much. I never thought they muddled them over much, but the more attention was directed to them, the more Les Burbage seemed to come to mind—and so we grew up in a temperance town in a temperance state, and while all of us were moderate, I'm sure none of us was ever excessively one or the other, and all of us were discerning and tolerant. Tolerance, even, was one of Les Burbage's own lessons—because I've heard him say dozens of times, "If a man wants to stay sober, he's got a right to, I always say."

A MORE modern sociological approach seems to find the old Poor Farm an objectionable solution to what is otherwise a distressing problem, but the truth was that our Poor Farm was a good place and did its job well. We used to go up there for parties, and I kissed my first girl in the pantry there and got a molasses cookie at the same time. It was a fine cookie, about six inches across, and the recipe for them was known in my town as the Poor Farm Cookie. It was quite chewy, and there was a trick about cooking them in a slow oven, but there never was a finer cookie. Mabel Pitcher was the girl, and her father was keeper of the Town Farm, and she felt around in the dark and got me this special reward for what was not on the whole an objectionable experience. We were playing post-office.

It wasn't every town did it, but our town always made the Poor Farm a paying proposition, and it may be revealing that our folks were able to show a profit on the welfare account. They were that kind of people, although you are right—they have been badgered and bewildered by modern ideals and ideas until they have sold the farm and started regarding the poor as a liability like any modern self-respecting civil division. In my youth this was not so, and our Poor Farm was such a fine place that we were proud of it all around, and thought the people who lived there were doing a good job.

The financial transactions concerned in the management of the farm were a marvel of civic bookkeeping, and the Selectmen carried everything under two accounts—one was "Poor In" and the other was "Contingent." The Town did most of its business under the contingent fund, and I have an annual report of the municipal officers that shows business over $28,000 on an appropriation of only $200. It is all honest and above-board, and quite understandable. The Selectmen merely did all they could under contingent, and put the rest somewhere else. We had businessmen for Selectmen, not bookkeepers. It is much better, now that the state auditor helps the towns, because insolvency has set in frequently enough to be chronic, and nobody can understand the accounts any more. I have never been able to understand the mental attitudes of accountants, who believe nothing is correct if anybody can understand it. Our old Selectmen wanted us to know how well they were doing, and how well we were doing, so they made everything a contingency. The Poor In account had to do with the town poor who were "in" the almshouse, as distinguished from the Poor Out, who were maintained in other ways—usually by grocery orders and free rent in a house the town had taken over for taxes. Like the Slades. The Slades "ran out" for some reason, and the generation in my time had eight children and few prospects beyond an annual increase in that number. So the town took over their home because they hadn't paid the taxes, and they went right on living there just the same, and when they didn't have enough money to eat, the town would give them a grocery order. When it came time to paint the house, the town would buy the paint and Mr. Slade would paint his house just the same as the Slades always had. It seems to me it was a good way, and spared the Slades the stigma of going on relief.

The other way to spare the paupers this stigma was to send them up to the Poor Farm, which was seldom called the Poor Farm but was properly identified as the Town Farm, with the heavier stress on the word Town. There they had good rooms, plenty to eat, and some employment according to their ability. The employment always resulted in a profit, and even in its worst years, our Town Farm broke even. I can see why—too. The farm was a good one, perhaps as good as any in town. It was fun to farm it, and we had plenty of good families in town who would take it over whenever the incumbent keeper failed to show good management. Since farming has become recognized as a type of work, this attitude has declined. My father was always the first to get Golden Bantam corn into the markets in our town, but the Town Farm was always second, and every pauper there worked hard all summer to try and beat us. One year they planted a white corn, which was a good enough corn except for its color, and word went around that my father had at last taken a back seat. But the white corn matures earlier anyway, and everybody knew that was a poor way to win, and although everybody bought some Town Farm corn that year, they stopped as soon as my father got to market the next week. But the fields of corn at the Town Farm were beautiful, and even the elderly cripples there played some part in the harvests. Everybody had a job. In the winter they hooked rugs, the women poking the hooks through and making patterns, and the men all sitting around with shears cutting up old suits.

These parties we had were wonderful. Mabel used to like to give birthday parties, and her mother was the kind who didn't mind whipping up a freezer of cream, a few cakes, some cookies, and a hundred or so sandwiches. Mabel's own birthday was something we children looked forward to, but Mabel would also give parties for some of the rest of us. We would hike out to the place, going up the long lane under the elms and maples, and arriving in a gang. Mabel's family ran both up and down, and her father was a great big happy-faced man with a long black moustache. He had the most magnificent moustache cup I ever saw, with a full-bosomed mermaid on it, and in gold letters it said, "Souvenir of New Bedford, Mass." He bought it at an auction, and had never been to New Bedford. Besides the Pitchers, the Town Farm kitchen would have four or five of the Town Farm people there—some of them invalids of a sort, but most of them ordinary people we knew about town, good friends to us all. It being common knowledge that not everybody runs at the same speed, it stood to reason any town would have poor people, and it wasn't always their fault. As Town Farm people, they were doing something to help themselves along, and they had as much right to go to Mabel's birthday party as anybody.

They would, however, wander off to bed after supper dishes were done, and even those who stayed later for the party would leave before we children really got going. The party was just like any of our parties. We played games and ate. That isn't important, but I think it is important that the Town Farm and the people at it figured in a childhood party. It shows a sociability prevailed that hasn't outlived that time, mostly because the Town Farm hasn't outlived it. People who say the Town

Farm was a barbarous way to deal with a human problem are full of prunes. The Town Farm was a good place, and since our town sold it, people have said a thousand times it was a poor thing to do. Now the poor cost money, they are still poor under any other name, and they don't have the homey atmosphere of the big Town Farm kitchen and they don't have that chance to pay their own way.

They did pay their own way. The man before Mabel's father had been keeper for 25 years, and as a provider for the unhappy poor he had more head on him than all the modern social workers put together. His annual appearance at Town Meeting was a triumph of governmental wonder. His report, showing how much money the farm had made the previous year, had been published in the annual printed report, but he had saved the pertinent details for his speech to the voters. It is long since I heard him. I used to have a tray of cigars and eating tobacco to sell, which was a good way to earn a penny while learning about this democracy thing in the greenhouse where it grows. This was before votes for women, and the men put out their pipes and made Town Meeting an excuse to smoke cigars. In this vaporous arena Henry MacLean would take the floor to make his Town Farm Speech. I hope my memory does some kind of justice to his remarks:

> *Mr. Moderator: Gentlemen—The report this year needs to be amplified in some particulars, but not a hell of a lot. The team was put out a total of 45 days on gravel and snow, as you can see, but that team don't work too well on the ro'd, and I hope to swap 'em off next year, if I live, and get something more rugged. I'd like to consider the money they made last year as available to buy a new team, and while I'll keep the old one if you say so, I think you ought to figure on a change. Now the woodlot income ain't*

up to what I'd like, but if you people are going to buy wood from the shipyard and sawmills, you got to put up with it. If you'll give me your wood orders before the first of June, and put up some part of the amount, it will help a great deal, and I can take care of about a hundred cords without any trouble, and have enough money ahead to get a new team for yarding. I wasn't planning to commence hauling wood until around Labor Day, but I was talking to Stumpy Hudson here this morning, and he says he d'know-but he'll put in to come up with us, and if he does, I'll put him right to yarding wood, because he's handy with a team, and we may get to it sooner. I was kinder hoping to have somebody could do teaming, but the way it's been the last few years with mostly women and old men, I had to do the teaming all myself, as you know and no need to go into that again. We have to do with what we got. Well, I got seed enough for ten acres potatoes, so there won't be no need to put up seed money at all. I was figuring on saving seed money and putting the same amount to a team if that's agreeable. I do want to sow down quite a piece to grass this year, and that may make a difference in haying time, as I may have to hire a hand or two for a week or so. The small garden last year was the best damn garden in town, and you can see how we cleared on it by the report. We raised all our own vegetables and berries, and gave away a lot we couldn't sell. Some of the poor people in town was glad for the help we gave them, and while that don't show up anywhere as income, you people all know how it happened, and will make allowances. One woman, and I don't mind saying it was Mrs. Jane Whitcher, picked 76 quarts of blueberries all by herself, and they was quite a batch of raspberries got, *too. Those things count up, and come in handy. I guess that's about all, except to call your attention to the regular written report. Now it don't make no damn's odds to me how you vote, and you do as you're a mind to, but I think you ought to allow for the boot on a new team, and seeing how those old horses have been going down hill, it may run into quite a bit before we get to it. I'd like to make a motion, Mr. Moderator, that we raise and appropriate the sum of $300 for poor in for the ensuing year, on the understanding that we can draw on the contingent fund if we decide to get a new team. I thank you kindly.*

This was really quite a speech for anybody to make in Town Meeting, and had become the regular thing because of Henry's great pride in the good work he was doing for the Town Farm. The $300 asked for was, actually, in the nature of a loan, because by the end of the financial year Henry would have balanced it off, and more. There was never a murmur about the appropriation—in fact, somebody would usually get up and make a little speech, extolling Henry's care of the inmates, his great application to his work, and the excellence of his comprehensive reports. In short, while the whole thing doesn't mean much today, it was the way our town covered the business details of caring for the poor. The new team of horses were bought, and Stumpy Hudson did go to the Town Farm to drive them, and at the next regular meeting of the Town, it was reported that the Poor In account had been able to show a net profit of $700, not counting the new carry-over of seed potatoes. This took care of two burials, too, which was unusual, because the folks at the Town Farm got such good care that hardly any of them ever died short of the 90's, and had such a good time none of them wanted to.

There was one summer that the Town Farm folks planted a big field of beans for a canning factory, and word went out that they needed pickers to get the crop harvested before the beans "went by." The boys of the town turned out, and it was understood we were to get 1¢ a pound for picking. During the course of the work, somebody said he didn't intend to take his money. "My father said it would be a good thing to donate this work, where it's for the town." This struck us as a fine idea, and we all announced that we were picking beans gratis. The "boss" of the picking was this same Stumpy Hudson, who had a twisted leg as well as a somewhat twisted intellect, and we all took orders from him and thought nothing of it. When word got around that the boys were picking beans for nothing, some of the girls joined in, and Stumpy had to boss us pretty hard because a mixed bean crew sometimes gets its mind on other things besides beans. After that, some of the parents thought it would be a good business to help, and when Sunday came there were almost more pickers than there were beans, and Stumpy was hopping around over the patch bossing until he was red in the face. He combed out some of the town's better businessmen for getting hard beans in the bags, and lectured on the difference between Number Ones and Number Twos, which is mainly a degree of growth. The chief result of this was a great community interest in the Town Farm, and for years after that bean venture the voters were very generous with the budget, and bought such things as new furniture, milk equipment, several new pieces of farm machinery, and eventually gave Henry MacLean a purse of money and a fine new Hamilton watch when he retired. Henry, who had run the Town Farm for so long, retired from active management, and continued to live there, and basked happily in the reflections of his career while Mabel's father took over and tried to do as well.

I can remember, while more modern philosophies echo in my ears as well, how proud Mabel and her brothers and sisters used to be when they would tell people, "We live at the Town Farm!" It was a good place to live, and it was probably the best place I ever knew of to go for a birthday party. Those molasses cookies haunt me still, and I guess we youngsters used to envy those poor inmates who could have them any time they liked.

In CASTING back over affairs in my town when I was a boy, I have fished up a great many random yarns and remarks that have no particular place in even this random chronicle, but the format of publication is not too good a mold for the variegated happenings of boyhood, and somehow everything fits even when it doesn't—and somehow the morals are felt the most when they are most obscure.

I wouldn't, for instance, know just where to fit in Mason Thurlow, who had lived a busy life and came finally to the time when he was nothing much beyond the visiting committee for the Knights of Pythias. Whenever a brother was sick, Mason would take his half-bushel basket of fruit and cookies and jellies and candy, and go and call. This was the same thing as an official visitation from the lodge, and Mason had his own way of brightening the dismal period of recuperation. In the midst of a blizzard,

178

one winter, his oranges and nuts shielded from the snow by a newspaper cover, Mason struggled through the drifts to the home of Ralph Goodridge, who was laid up with something. Puffing from the exertion, Mason stomped his feet on the porch and came in, walking into the bedroom with his overcoat and hat on, and sat down beside the bed.

"God sakes, Ralph," he puffed, "Why'n't you get somebody to shovel out that drive—how do you think we'll get the hearse in?"

In later years when Mason himself lay stark and cold in his casket, almost every Knight of Pythias in town smiled down at the bier, because all of them had been treated to just such a cheer-up visit from the old codger. He was always measuring the bedroom door to see if they could carry out the corpse two-and-two, or remarking how a coffin in the bow-window would show up well from the street. And his parting remark had been, probably a thousand times, as he ended his visit and started to go, "After you're gone, I'll come back for the basket, baskets are hard to get, and I like that one." That's about all there was to it, and Mason played his little part in the village.

Then we had a very pompous man who moved into town in later years, and he was said to be able to "strut sitting down." One day he was in Meggett's store, and Mr. Meggett was arranging a special display of canned peaches. Mr. Meggett was a great hand to buy some such item in quantity, when he could get a price, and run a special sale and clean it all out in a day or so. It was good old-time merchandising, and brought everybody into his store so he had a chance to let them see his other stock and sometimes the items he bought were more for show than for sale. But this sale of canned peaches was a good one, and everybody stocked up for winter, and Mr. Meggett was just in the act of building a huge pyramid of the cans in the middle of his store. It was a tremendous pile, wide at the bottom and coming to a peak at the ceiling, and Mr. Meggett was on a ladder braced against a beam just in the act of laying on the top-most can when this pompous man, Archer Babcock, came strutting into the store and stumbled bang against the corner of the pyramid.

The noise was something to hear. The rumble and bumping went on, it seemed, for an interminable time, and the cans kept falling long after you'd have thought every last one of them had been flat on the floor. The doors of the store were open, and people came running from all up and down the street. As the last vibration died away and the crowd gathered, there was this shambles of peach cans all over the store floor, with Mr. Babcock standing in the middle of them with his chest stuck out, and there was Mr. Meggett up on the ladder with one can still outstretched in his hand.

Mr. Babcock said, "Well, Mr. Meggett, I guess we didn't break anything."

Mr. Meggett said, "No, but it was more by good luck than good wit." And then Mr. Meggett started selling peaches to the crowd, and all the rest of the day you could see people going home with big bags full of the cans, and the pompous man was always known after that as Good Luck Archer.

Or there was Cap'n Bruce MacDougal, who always cut up the meat for people who ate at his house. Most hosts just serve, and the guest has to do his own work. But Cap'n MacDougal would say, "When you eat to my house, you just eat." He'd smash the boiled potato, put butter on it, coat it with gravy. He'd slice the roast, and then cut the slice up into bite sizes, push it to one side, and heap on the greens, and peas and beans. It took forever for him to serve a table full, but he kept talking and telling stories while he did it, and eating at his house was no work at all.

He knew all the personal likes and dislikes of his guests, such as who took mustard on his meat and who didn't like cabbage, and he even put on pepper and salt for those he was sure of. When he got through, all you had to do was eat. A lot of people didn't believe this, and some of them finagled an invitation to supper, and came away saying it was so. Once at a Grange supper the ladies fixed it so the captain sat at the head of a table, and he spent the whole evening fixing supper for the 25 or 30 people at that table, and the thing then became a matter of public knowledge. He even took your piece of apple pie, crunched it gently with the side of a fork, and poured on cream for you, and would sugar and stir your coffee.

We had a lot of men around town who did women's work with neatness and proficiency, without stirring up an iota of thought about it. Aaron Yeakson hemmed up skirts, and was known all over town as the best hemmer there was. He liked to do it. You could see a woman going over to his house with some dressmaking in a box and Aaron would stand them on a chair and go around them with pins, and the next day he'd have it all done and wouldn't take a cent. Aaron was a whiskery old man who had been a teamster all his life, and he took up needlework the way some people would take up stamp collecting or writing bad poetry. Then there was Herman Gratham, who did needlepoint, much the same way. He didn't do anything with it when he got it done. He'd make a piece, and then make another. They had an exhibition of his things in the library one time, and everybody admired them and wanted to buy some, but Herman wouldn't sell. I suppose he still has it, because he's still living and I imagine is still making needlepoint. But the most universal masculine assumption of woman's work in our town was the ability to cook. I don't imagine my town ever turned out a man who didn't, one time or another, master a good wood range and memorize the basic recipes. I doubt if there's a small-town man in Maine today who can't bake as good biscuits as his wife. They don't all run to fancy things, but on plain cooking they can get along. A few months ago some people came to call on me at the farm, and I apologized because the family was away and asked them to wait a minute while I took a pie out of the oven. It came to me all at once that these visitors thought I was simply wonderful to be doing such a thing, but the truth is that all us boys picked up the art to some degree or another. Many a time I've heard, "You'd make somebody a good wife" when some of the menfolks in my town had turned out a meal. Some of the men were experts beyond the women themselves. There was a potato salad the women wished they could match, and no Grange supper was whole unless Ralph Foster had contributed. Carl Robbins was a dabster at frosting a cake, and if you brought the sugar he'd make a masterpiece for a dollar. Carl had been a cook at sea for a time, but of course he never frosted any cakes under sail.

Now I think all these things have morals to them, somewhere. There was a story about little John Brewster when he was in school and they came to physics. The teacher did her best to explain centrifugal and centripetal force, and everybody was trying hard to understand. The teacher then asked Johnnie what kind of a vehicle would negotiate a corner safest at a high speed. I don't know what the answer was supposed to be, but John's answer was, "A stone drag." This unexpected jointure of stark reality and the axioms of physical inertia tickled the fancy of the town, and John's remark became a legend. Whenever anybody asked a foolish question, he was sure to get the answer—"A stone drag." Once in Town Meeting the superintendent of schools was arguing for some proposition, and he ended with a rhetorical question, "And so

I ask you, etc., what better method has been proposed, and so forth." Ike Fowler jumped up and shouted, "A stone drag!" and the measure was defeated with a great show of parliamentary courtesy. You can still get a laugh in my town by saying, "A stone drag!"

There was a great deal of pure literary nonsense, too, which is a good thing for a boy to grow up with. There was a fellow who, somehow, started the notion that he had a setting hen in his whipsocket on his buggy. To heighten this complete illusion, he carried his buggy whip in his hand, and everywhere he went people would come over and look down into the whipsocket and inquire for the hen. "When's she due off?" became the watchword with that, and the thing went along until it died a natural death.

Or we had the by-word from Liz Merrill's buggy ride. Somebody saw her along the road one day, her horse up on the banking chewing poplar leaves, and Liz walloping him with a stick. One buggy wheel was on a stone wall, another on a stump, and the whole thing was precarious. "What in the world are you doing, Liz?" the man called out, and Liz made history by saying, "Well, I'm *trying* to get to town." And forever and ever, I hope folks in my town will greet any moment of utter frustration with a grin and the remark, "I'm trying to get to town." Liz, poor soul, has been dead three generations, but her noble try lives on.

Now these things developed out of the pattern of life, and they were not the he-and-she anecdotes of the comic magazines. We had a native ability to see the humor in our own good way, and every opportunity was embraced. We had, too, the magnificent capacity for poetry of the down-coast State o'Mainer, and I wouldn't want to try evaluating my boyhood without speaking of it. Because it is thoroughly true that Maine people live a wondrous poetry that will never be set down for the pious to read. It is a poetry over and above the poetry of the fastidious, for much of it is unfit to print. But it is poetry, all the same. It is poetry so long as you communicate in figures and images, allow for the melody of words, and grant that ideas shall be expressed. I wish the postal laws might be lifted long enough for some appreciative person to set down in one asbestos-bound volume the real poetry of the Maine coast—for it is beautiful in an abandoned sort of way, and it is expressive as any muse could hope for.

I can't give any examples, owing to the stringent restrictions of the mails, and the moral outlook of less poetic people. But the flair for poetry that gives us so many decent Maine expressions extends beyond what is polite. Up to that point, we have the genius for metaphor that no other people anywhere, as far as I know, ever matched. A lobster boat, in Maine, is never just plain "tight," signifying that its carpentry is precise enough to frustrate leaking. To ordinary people in ordinary places, a boat would be tight. But in Maine a boat is always "tight's a cup." The image comes through, and that is poetry. If the boat leaks —she "leaks like a lobster pot." And as the slatted sides of a lobster trap were intended to allow a maximum passage of water, the image has again come through. It was this imagery that gave us Hannah Cook. Hannah has become a legend—an obscure one, because strangers believe that Hannah was a woman, and that she was useless. "That cultivator ain't worth a Hannah Cook," may be the way it runs. Hannah, however, was not a woman. In the early sailing days when men signed into a crew, each had his category based on his experience and ability. One man might be a mate, another might be a cook. The ordinary foremast hand was simply "a hand." And to round out the crew, every master shipped some nondescript seaman who signed as "hand or cook." Such had no special category, and were usually unequal to certified position. So they weren't much good. And whatever wasn't much good came to be likened to a "hand or cook," and the Hannah Cook of the adage was merely the practical fruition of what was originally poetic imagery.

The same with Charlie Noble. The British Admiralty records that an American (obviously, of course, Maine) merchant master around 1800 discovered at sea, one day, that his galley stovepipe was brass, and delighted with this unusual fact he gave orders that it should be kept bright. So he sailed the world around, and whenever a bright brass smoke pipe was seen at sea, everybody knew Cap'n Charles Noble was at hand. And Charlie Noble became a synonym for a stovepipe, and by extension a synonym for any stack or chimney, and the imagery took and stuck. What poet first made the comparison and the transfer of values has been lost forever. Indeed, Cap'n Charles has almost been lost. But a Charlie Noble is a galley stovepipe wherever the tides run, and the poetry is with us still. In that expression is summed up the frivolous, comical, vain, whimsical and whatnot incongruity of a shining stovepipe, and I really believe it was a man from my town who first summed it. Through all our speech, when I was a boy, ran this sort of thing, and my mother pointed out to me that Maine people don't talk with words—they talk with ideas. So, indeed, does a poet—and so, I think, we were all poets. And good ones. And we lived our ways and talked about what we lived, and repeated our by-words and tag-lines, and a boy growing up was bound to get something out of it.

We had a story about the evangelist who asked his audience to rise if they wanted to go to heaven. They all rose except one man. So the minister asked those who wanted to go to hell to stand up. Nobody stood. So the minister fixed his pulpit gaze of scorn on this non-participating man and asked him where he wanted to go. The man said, "Nowhere, I like it here." It was this spirit that prompted our people, back when the expression came to us from bragging excursionists—you remember it, the satisfied one would say—"Oh, I've been around." This was probably true, and the person who had been around mistook travel and experience for the pure essence of Knowledge. Our folks, who had certainly been around as much as anybody, lost no time in supplying the poetic answer.

They would say, "So's the button on the backhouse door." No poet, couched comfortably in the thickest of anthologies, ever got more into one line. It was the way with us. We liked it there. It was no particular achievement to have been around. Didn't foolish Joe Mingo be around in his time? He lived 87 years, and all but nine of them were spent on board or in port, and he still didn't know anything when he died.

But these random stories and sayings were part of our growing up, and from each we gained something that rounded our perceptions. Knowledge is the accumulation of many things, and usually they are little things and random. And I guess they are always things that formal education ignores. The old timers in my town did things and said things, and did them their way and said them their way—and never knew they were teachers.

Saunders

I<small>N</small> THOSE days food ran largely to nourishment, which
was considered a good thing, and our mothers were first
of all good cooks. The day has passed, and no matter how
many women in these times can load down a table, they
don't do it with the ease and genius that prevailed back
then. Some of the difference is a matter of attitude, because our ideas about living have changed, but in those
days the sea and land conspired to provide an abundance
of raw materials, and the stores had not been corrupted
by packaged and processed improvements. Somehow nicety
had not developed so the cat asleep in the store window
among the unwrapped goods was looked upon askance,
and the alimentary tract still felt it had a job to do to earn
its keep. Nobody had told our stomachs about vitamins
and calories, and we thought it was far more important to
have something to eat. We were awful ignorant then,
but we ate well and took pleasure in it.

Not long ago a great and splendid self-service chain store advertised that special baby buggies had been added to the equipment so mother's little darling could be wheeled about while mother selected from the pre-packaged shelves whatever goodies her larder required. Thus does the modern age reach into the very cradle with its insidious propaganda and conditioning, and a youngster can't help growing up into a chain-store addict. I grew up otherwise, and I am glad.

Our storekeeper was Mr. Philoon, who seldom looked through the square spectacles he wore down on his nose or up on his forehead. Trading with him was a social event, and there was no little buggy to ride around in while looking for goods. Mother didn't look for goods. Mr. Philoon knew where they were, and he got them for her. Usually he knew what Mother wanted before she asked. I deplore the dispatch and speed of modern marketing. We went in leisurely, shopped leisurely, and came out the same way. Mr. Philoon, wiping his hands on his butcher's apron, would come from the back room where he had been corning beef. He corned his own beef, and I would like to have a piece now. I don't know where chain stores corn their beef, or if they corn any. I am not interested. Mr. Philoon greeted my mother with the customary, "What can I do you for?" which was supposed to be very humorous, and an introduction to the pleasant chat that would follow. Mother would say that she didn't know what she wanted. Mr. Philoon would open the back of his candy case and fish me out a jawbreaker—or maybe a candy fried egg in a tin spider with a tiny tin spoon for eating it. I knew how to be careful, because I had already cut my lip on the spoons many times. Penny candy, then, sometimes came two and three for a cent, but it wasn't every day we had a cent. Mr. Philoon knew what he was doing, and he wouldn't have dared to forget.

"How about a piece of pork, could you go pork?"

"It's pretty hot for pork, I guess not."

Mr. Philoon had already started to cut off some steak, and I suppose Mother knew as well as he did that she would take steak when all was said and done. He inquired if we had tomatoes. We used to put tomatoes in his store and always took back what he didn't sell. The hens would eat them, and Mr. Philoon wasn't saddled with a doubtful investment. We'd do the same with chain stores today if they had sense enough to buy local produce with some display of enthusiasm, but they prefer to ship things in from far places and dump what spoils. Mr. Philoon liked to have us "take things out in trade." It gave him a two-way crack at the profits, besides making for good customer relations. In those days when a storekeeper spoke of "good will" he really had some.

We paid Mr. Philoon every two weeks. If Father paid, he got a cigar, but when Mother paid she would bring home a five-cent bar of candy as a treat, or sometimes a striped bag of crystal-cream candies that came in a wooden pail and have since been forgotten as the world thought it was improving. Then my father would go over the slips and see if Mr. Philoon had made any mistakes in his addition, and he often had. Mr. Philoon wasn't too accurate at ciphering, and he erred both ways after no particular system. He wasn't offended when you showed him a mistake, and would say, "Mistakes do happen, spite of me." He always rectified the error by making the amount the first item on the next set of slips. He knew we'd continue to trade there. People didn't very often get mad and "take their trade across the street."

But Mr. Philoon's store had things to eat in it. The cheese case had cheese and the molasses barrel had molasses. Bananas came by the bunch and he cut off what you wanted until the denuded stalk hung there and it was time to hang a new bunch. Cellophane was yet to be discovered by a mad scientist. The pickle barrels were attended by their little glass dippers with drain-holes in the bottom, and when we had a cent we would go in and buy a pickle and fish with the dipper until we really found a big one. The age of popsicles is an effete age—we walked to school sucking salt-water cucumbers and puckered up everybody we met. It was a wooden barrel and pine crate age, and corrugated cartons were ahead of us. There were a few prepared breakfast cereals then, but Mother told me they were for hot weather, and we ate oatmeal and cornmeal. If some magnificent man with his heart a-dream should wish to favor humanity today by running a store like Mr. Philoon's, of course he couldn't. The goods are not available. The public has been misled into newer habits. The enterprise would be looked upon as a freak— something for tourists and city folks to oh and ah at. But when we had stores like Mr. Philoon's, we had a great beginning for our hearty moments around the dinner table. It was merely the beginning, and what Mother did was far more important, but our kind of bringing-up needed a Mr. Philoon and the thought and doings that went with him, and with his era.

It is too easy to sit back and roll off wonderful accounts of big Sunday and holiday feasts, when the families gathered and demolished terrific appetites. But the truth is that we ate much that way all the time. Our breakfasts were intended to see us through until noon, when dinner came. The whole firm structure of American life changed when dinner was politely changed to lunch. A lunch was something we occasionally packed in a half-bushel basket to take on a picnic, but we never ate a lunch of any kind while seated at a table. Dinner was a noonday meal, and it consisted mainly of meat and potatoes and pie, and it was generally believed that if you didn't eat a good dinner you had something the matter with you and needed a tonic. When I was pumping the organ in the church and wasted away, Father thought I needed a tonic to build me up, and before every meal I had to take a spoonful of stout, which I didn't particularly like. Father, as he poured me my spoonful, joined me with a small glass of it, and while I put on weight with some speed, my father gained 37 pounds in no time and Mother made us stop. Supper came in the evening at supper time and it wasn't too different from dinner except that we usually had sauce instead of pie. Sauce, to us, was a dish of preserved fruit of some kind; strawberries, plums, peaches, pears. And sometimes fresh fruit. A dish of cut-up fruit was a wonderful supper sauce, and I was dismayed when I learned in later years that it had been moved to the head of the meal and was called a fruit cup. I would like the fruit cup at swank banquets if they would make it three sizes bigger and keep it for last. I will never approve of having dessert first, because Mother taught us we should never eat things just before supper.

Or we had puddings for supper. Chocolate custards, pieces of cake bathed in lemon sauce—that kind of pudding. Indian puddings were common then, and they had more wallop to them sometimes than the meal itself. Pan dowdies. And "concoctions." "Mother's made a concoction!" we children would shout, and everybody would try it to see if it was good. It always was, but Mother never remembered the exact proportions, and we never had the same concoction twice.

There was an unauthorized and ex officio fourth meal, which was called, "Something to eat." Before we went to bed. "I want something to eat," was preliminary sometimes to quite a hearty meal, with the tea things and knives and forks, but more often it stopped at raiding the cookie jar or the doughnut crock, or maybe finishing up the spice cake with the raspberry frosting. I want to be accurate about this, and I'm not sure I can't construe a fifth meal as well, which came after school, or about that time in the summer, and was usually a slice of new bread with molasses spread clear out to the crusts and the whole thing covered with a layer of brown sugar. I think that might be considered a meal by the modern generation of lady-like appetites. We ate it on the run. Six or eight of us would line up in some pantry, not always our pantry, and some mother would patiently cut and spread until we all had a piece, and then we would light out off the back steps and leave the screen door to slam and we'd eat as we went. I have heard that calm and relaxation are supposed to be the best assistants to effective ingestion of nourishment, but as an old bread-and-molasses-and-brown-sugar gourmet I feel this may not be so. We assimilated at a high rate of speed, and I think the digestion process is more adaptable than the specialists think.

None of the things we ate were loudly acclaimed as "good for us." We were expected to finish our milk, but it was uncouth and barbaric milk, because it had never been processed under sanitary conditions at great expense, and I doubt if that kind of milk can be counted today. We had greens and salads, but they weren't prescribed for health reasons, and I gather we ate them because we liked them, or refused to eat them if we didn't. We brought home watercress from the trout brooks, gathered fiddle-head ferns, boiled mustard greens, and made sea-moss puddings. Somewhere along the line we seemed to get enough to live on, and we weren't too much impressed with items we didn't care for—no matter how "good for us" they might have been.

There was an abiding belief in the efficacy of cooking things. We ate a lot of stews and boiled meat was good. We had boiled dinners, always with a chunk of salt pork to marry with the brisket. It was leisurely cooking in the cordwood days, and it was contrary to all the fine modern belief that the goodness can be cooked out of things. People today don't cook things, they frighten them with heat. Our carrots and onions and potatoes and turnips and cabbage and meat were in the pot long enough so they really got acquainted with one another, and when they came out they were all singing the same tune and had quite a program lined up. Nobody with the welfare of the human race at heart would ever try to cook a boiled dinner in one of these pressure chambers with a steam gauge on top. It is a question of time. It takes long association to make a lamb stew, and you can't expect a group of people to start right in being intimate after the first introductory handshake. Nodding acquaintance among the ingredients never made a lamb stew. Vegetables, also, tend to be reserved until they have allowed a friendship to ripen and are willing to dispense with formality. A stew based on individuality may be healthful, and may be chock-o-block full of fine, high-quality, upstanding vitamins, but its flavor is nothing to make a man love his mother the way I love mine. Mother cooked things.

Better than that, Mother knew that a good part of her destiny in life was to cook things. She liked to cook. She knew, if she'd stopped to analyze it, that woman hath no greater love than to lay down a good meal at the proper time, and that reciprocation of such affection is a foregone conclusion. There is much in a gingerbread that the experts have neglected. I am in favor of rewriting the marriage vows so they will read, ". . . to love, cherish, obey and bake gingerbread until death us do part." My boyhood was a gingerbread boyhood, with glasses of cold milk, and I know that the stomach has been overlooked as the seat of the emotions and the stabilizer of domestic harmony. The heart and the head are capricious, but a comfortable stomach endureth all things and will continue to admire and adore. My mother never said as much in any of her instructive remarks, but she knew it, and she proved that she was right. Incompatibility, which has become a tragic social problem, would evaporate into nothingness if a raspberry pie could be inserted into the unhappy household at the critical moment. Songs would be sung again, and hearts would be joyful, and abiding affection would set in and prevail.

Anyway, food was abundant in my boyhood, and good —and we learned of its importance. We were bulk customers. We had our fish chowders and beef stews and watermelon-rind pickles and oatmeal and fried eggs and custard sauce and raisin pies and appetite was a recurring excuse to have more. And we never got so fastidious we inquired into chemical contents. If it tasted good we ate it and were glad. And it did taste good, because our whole social importance was predicated on mealtime as a hallowed moment. "Don't care what you call me, so long as you don't call me late to dinner!" was the way the expression ran. I have missed many of life's more celebrated opportunities and have survived thus far intact and unworried. But I have not yet missed a meal, and as this was the predominant item in my education, it is the only field in which I am proud of my marks.

I GOT 25¢ a week for pumping the organ in the church, and it wasn't bad until we had a new minister come and he took his work seriously. Ministers are funny, sometimes, and seem to quarrel a good deal with sin. My idea now is that ministers wouldn't have much to do if everybody was holy, and they ought to be glad we're wicked, but as a boy I still had my perceptions to sharpen, and I pumped with enthusiasm while they sang all six verses of several hymns in the worthy task of bringing my generation to redemption. I pumped so hard my folks noticed I was wasting away to skin and bones, and they called a halt. The program went ahead without me, but not until I had surveyed the mysteries of divine worship from my vantage point in the organ loft.

I think the older folks in the congregation were puzzled by this new minister. We always had an old minister —one who had exhausted the fires of enthusiasm long ago, and had settled down to the routine of two sermons and a prayer meeting weekly, sick calls, and whatever he could do to keep out of trouble. This new minister was younger, and he felt an urgency upon him. I think he made the customary mistakes, the only difference being that he made them in our town and we'd never seen them before.

Most new ministers seem to think the nature of their work implies a good deal of assistance will come from above, and that personal exertion is much less necessary than in mundane professions like plumbing, dressmaking, and undertaking. This is a delusion, as God seems no more interested in His own vicars than He is in any other business, and the ministers shortly observe this. A sense of futility sets in, and it leads usually to proclaiming from the pulpit that the younger generation is going to Hell. This is probably true, but it is nothing any generation doesn't do, and it never seems sporting to make an issue of it. My generation certainly did, and yours either did or will, and my pet belief is that Sunday evening church services promote more sin than salvation. From an organ loft you can watch the boys tear leaves out of the hymn books, slowly so the rip won't disturb the evening lesson, and write notes to pass to the girls in the pews ahead. Such notes succeed in pairing everybody off for the walk home, and if you pump the organ you soon learn to make arrangements before the opening hymn, because you won't have any chance to join in the note passing from up there. Some evenings the minister and I were the only ones left to walk home alone, and I think the virtue of our contributions to spiritual guidance were too small a reward to represent fair return. I don't know how he felt, but I was sad.

Anyway, this minister damned the younger generation, and started a campaign to save us. The older folks seemed agreeable, although some of the boys felt, when summer came along, that Bible study was cutting in seriously on the baseball team. We had a good team at our church, and one year Ned Dunklin struck out the Baptists in three straight no-hit games. Ned's father ran the pool room, however, and the pool room was supposed to be unholy, and after the minister's program got under way Ned's father wouldn't let him come to church any more. Ned promoted a rebellion, and took our whole infield up and joined the Baptist Sunday School, where an elderly minister was abiding his time and would come out in the evening and coach hitting practice. Ministers who never were inside a pool room get funny ideas about them. It made some of the older folks take notice, though, when he scolded so much about the pool room that our baseball petered out. Nothing is so successful as a winning team.

After I gave up pumping the organ they got a foolish fellow to take over the job. There was no evident diminution in the quality of the music, but with Sunday nights at home I was able to improve my school work a lot, and I escaped the general migration into the fold of the church. The younger people, cowed by the sermons about their moral laxity, sought redemption eagerly, and the minister had a bigger and bigger group passing notes with the passage of every week. But the thing folded up when we played the Baptists on Saturday and the foolish fellow who pumped organ muffed a bunt on third and let three runs in. His name came up for membership that Sunday after the morning worship, and the members of the church blackballed him.

The minister jumped up and said it was most irregular, he'd never heard of anybody being refused admission to Christian fellowship. Deacon Justin Maybury also jumped up and said, "Well, you have now." The minister said if that was the case he would tender his resignation. Deacon Maybury got up and moved a committee to pass forward and receive the resignation, but the minister said it would take a day or two to word it properly. Anyway, the minster shortly moved on to another place. He said he'd had a "call," and my father said with God all things are possible. We got an older minister the next time, one who was so inured that he would fall asleep in his chair during the anthem, and Ned and the infield came back, and all of us were allowed to go to Hell unharried. Which, I guess, we did.

Naturally ours was a Congregational Church. That is the particular offshoot of the Reformation that received the benediction of the Massachusetts Bay Company when settlers on our New England shores first felt the need of spiritual leadership. Actually, it was more political than churchly, and is tied up in our Town Meeting system. Each parish was its own boss, just as each Town was largely sovereign. In those early days the Meeting House, or Town House, was the church. Members of the Town were members of the Parish, and those who paid poll taxes were allowed to vote in both. The desire to tax themselves to support a minister was usually the reason given for wishing a charter as a Town. It thus came about that New England was covered with "First Parish Churches"—indicating that these parishes were the lineal descendants of the first religious efforts of the Town. And even today it does not follow that a member of the parish is a member of the church. The parish maintains the church, and meets to appropriate money for it. The parish regulates the conduct of the church, handles the money and pays the bills. The church is a religious society within the parish. As other denominations came into the scene, the original distinctions became obscure, but even yet our First Parish meets and conducts the business of the church.

There's more to it than that, but I explain this much to introduce the parable of the minister from Maryland, who came up to our town to help us with our devotions, and shortly was informed that the parish would meet on Monday night next. This interested him, but without knowing a thing of the political background, he attended. It shortly seemed to him that something on the agenda demanded his comment, so he arose and addressed the meeting with logic and skill. He was reminded, however, that as he was not a member of the parish, his remarks were out of order. This is a terrible thing to have happen to a Marylander who is working hard among Maine people, and he was aghast. He pointed out that he was pastor of the church. Dave Morton told him that was quite a different organization, and when he spoke here it was the same as an Odd Fellow trying to talk to the Knights of Pythias. The minister asked if the matter might be explained to him. It took quite a time to do it, and then he said he still didn't understand. Hubert Weyland told him he was just like a hired hand in a shoe shop, sort of, and this was a directors' meeting. The minister finally gave up, and the parish meeting continued. My father was treasurer of the parish, but never belonged to the church. This was good, because my father would put the bee on everybody for a donation. "But I don't belong to your church," some of them would say. Father would say, "Neither do I," and he would usually get a donation. The Congregational Church therefore has in its concept of localized religious supremacy a fair feeling that it is the official community church. The notion is arrested considerably with changing times, particularly by other denominations, but The First Parish always has a leg-up when it comes to a discussion.

The thing that bothered the minister the most was the complete dual identity of members. Most folk belonged to both organizations, but each maintained loyalty to both and as parish members would brook no talking-down from the church. The minister conceded his position was untenable, but maintained the whole thing was absurd. He said the church ought to do away with the parish. My father said it would be more like it if the parish did away with the church. The minister didn't press the thing any further. Actually, however, from the standpoint of lawful procedure, my father was right. I gather the parish could kick the church out and open a hotel in the building if it wanted to. And in view of some of the things my townspeople have done, that's entirely within the realm of possibility.

You can see that growing up with my church gave me a wide and varied understanding of things, much more than the bare catechism and tenets of faith. In fact, I much fear the trappings and ceremony of devotions impressed me far less than some of the lore and legend I picked up along with them. I wouldn't want to be a man and not be able to remember the pageants, which were piously inspired, but enjoyed with impish eyes and ears. Once they had a magnificent Christmas spectacle in which the three orient wise men pursued a movable star down the center aisle, singing as they went in the darkened church, only the 50-watt star lighting their lock-step way. It was rehearsed until the center aisle carpet was almost worn out.

The mechanical star was fixed up by Percy Banter, who had a blacksmith shop and fixed bicycles. He took two bicycle wheels and mounted them at each end of the church, so a wire would fit around them and make pulleys. He had a gearing system in the choir loft so the bass could turn a crank and move the wheels. This moved the wire, and the wire carried the star. The thing squeaked a little in rehearsal, and Percy promised to oil it before the cantata. But the squeak gave somebody, forever unknown, an idea, and although Percy oiled it as he said he would, he was not the last person to work on it. Somebody reversed a couple of gears, thus sacrificing power to gain speed, and also fitted ratchets into the spokes.

The pageant was a great success up to the moment the wise men appeared. At the first words of their song, Fred Buxton began to turn the crank, and the Star of the East became a scintillating comet that streaked the length of the auditorium while the ratchets gave off like a boy dragging a stick on a picket fence. Mr. Buxton backed the comet off right away and adjusted his crank to the new gearing, but the damage was done. It was probably an extremely irreligious enjoyment that folks took in the spectacle, but it certainly was the most successful pageant we ever gave. Particularly when one of the wise men, in kneeling after his long trip, hitched his Magian costume a trifle too high and revealed that he hadn't rolled up his long-legged underwear quite as far as he thought he had.

I wonder now, of course, how I happened to come through my boyhood church experiences with any feeling for things of the spirit, or any knowledge of scripture. But I think I did, and I know most of us did. Very early in my life, my mother said, "I don't care what you make out of religion, but don't ever fail to support the church—some church." Her meaning seems to me to be sound, even if some may think she was suggesting a monetary attachment only. The truth is that we folks don't support anything without taking much interest in how it's run. I would rather let the thing rest there. The church I went to as a boy was a good church, and it gave me a lot of things it didn't know it was giving. And I got a lot I didn't know about at the time.

THE first time you dip your hand into the cold snow water of a Maine tidal stream and pick out a smelt, you are in for a surprise. A smelt is not slippery like other fish. He is as rough as sandpaper, and his stiffest wiggle helps him not. You can get hold of one by the merest trifle of his tail, and in spite of his struggle, you can hang on. It always seemed to me that nature had provided wisely for the benefit of small boys, because the small boys were never able to get a "set" on the smelt brooks, and the only way we could take any was by dipping for them with our numb and purple hands.

Smelting was one occasion when the older folks in our town seemed deficient in their attitudes toward us. We always went smelting, but unless we went as bag-holder for a father or older brother, we didn't get near the real fishing and had to content ourselves with hand-snatches. The real fishing was with nets, then, although our state officials have since limited the take to hook and line—except that dipping by hand has never had any legal status, for or against. Some day our state fisheries officials may get wise enough to know that fish are seldom depleted by fishing, but are ruined by unwise legislation, pollution, and forestry profligacy. I knew that long ago because on these smelting excursions I came to know Dr. Burgess, and he was one of the few men in the world who really knew about fish.

Smelting was a springtime matter, it came when the spring run-off was right. The sea-run smelts moved up into the fresh water with their seasonal urge, and time and season was such that we had the urge to go smelting at exactly the right time. It's funny about things like that. One day smelts are farthest from your mind, and then the moon is so-and-so, the wind gets thus-and-so, and something in the age-old mechanism of nature touches you up with the idea of smelts. It isn't a single instance. Everybody in town has it at the same time—just as the smelts have their own kind of urge at that time. One evening, everybody wanders down to his favorite smelt brook, and there you all are as if a notice had gone out. There wasn't a house in our town that didn't have a big smelt net stuck over the beams in the barn, and down it would come that afternoon for inspection and mending. A gunny sack, known better now as a burlap bag, would be tucked inside it, and with the long spruce pole of the net over his shoulder the householder would arrive to select his set.

A set was a place where rocks had been piled into the brook to direct the course of the up-coming smelts, and the gap fitted a net. These sets, built long ago and kept in annual repair, were spaced at intervals up and down the stream. On the coming tide, the smelts would move up the brook the way any sea-run fish comes in to spawn, and everybody stayed back away from the brook for a determined length of time. Thus the stretch of brook got filled with fish. Then the nets were put into the gaps in the rocks, and the entire length of the brook would be beaten with birch limbs to drive the smelts down, through the rocks, and into the nets. That's all there was to it. Sometimes a man would get all he could carry in one dip, and he'd go home and leave the set to somebody who came late.

The early comers got the best sets, of course. And we boys, most of us without nets, were ordered away from the stream lest we disturb the coming smelts and the routine of the catch. We were reduced, therefore, to a kind of poaching, and all we could do was sneak around with a lantern and look for random smelts and snatch them. Our sleeves rolled up in the cold spring night, and our arms to the elbows in the frigid water, we begged for pneumonia passionately—but we never got it. We did, however, get some smelts, and then later when we got bigger we got nets, and one night we finally got a set and joined the regulars.

Part of smelting was the bonfire. Back from the stream the men would kindle a blaze against a big log, and there we would all sit between "drives" to tell stories —and to listen to stories. The night tide was best for smelting, but the day tide also had something of a smelt run, and after a few nights I learned this. So I went down one afternoon to see what went on, and the brook looked ever so much different. The deep pools that reflected our lanterns and had no bottom were now fairly shallow. Here and there a smelt worked his way up through the pools, and when he came to one of the rock sets he could be snatched. I had a nice mess of smelts in no time—many more than I had ever got at night with a lantern. Those were not flashlight days, you see. The upper side of your lantern chimney would soot up, and you had to remember always to hold the thing right side down to get any light at all. You never really saw the smelt. You saw a thin black line in the water, usually not distinguishable from a rip in the water itself, and sometimes you made grabs for nothing at all. Sometimes, too, you got an eel which would wrap herself around your wrist and hang on. It was customary to throw the eels at somebody. You just hove them at a shadow in the dark, and one of the pleasures of smelting was to be looking into the water intently, and have an eel descend from nowhere at all and wrap herself around your neck with her tail stuck in your ear. This called for appropriate comments, and when these comments came everybody up and down the stream knew what had happened and burst into joyful hilarity. An eel has a slime on her body, and it comes off. When you have been hit with an eel, your clothes bear witness until the end of time. I used to have a big G right on the chest of my sweatshirt, where an eel twisted in that shape had hit me and dropped off in the water. The sweatshirt was washed regularly until it was tatters, but the G stayed.

But this afternoon when I was smelting by hand on the coming tide, I ran into Dr. Burgess, who was doing the same thing. Instead of a bag at his belt, he carried a bait pail, and each smelt was carefully placed in his pail. Every few minutes he dipped the pail in the stream to change the water. So we fell to talking, because Dr. Burgess was much given to instructing the boys, and he told me he was studying smelts. He asked me if I would let him clean my smelts.

Smelts don't always get cleaned, so this was an unusual request. At least half the people eat them just as they come from the water, and this is all right. My mother always claimed fish guts were intended to go to the hens, and we had ours cleaned, but plenty of people felt this was unbecoming fastidiousness and went ahead eating theirs in toto. But Dr. Burgess had a reason. I walked with him up to his laboratory.

Dr. Burgess actually was a doctor of medicine, but he had never practiced aside from an occasional first-aid job when he happened to be first on the spot. I saw him take off a man's finger once, after the man had come off second best with a bandsaw in the boatyard, and he looked just like any doctor as he did it. But he went into fisheries research early in life, and did so well at it that medicine lost him. His laboratory was actually a fisheries laboratory, and he had specimens from all over the world in it. He laid my smelts out on a board and began on them. Each fish was weighed and measured, a patch of his scales removed, and the entrails and scales were labeled. It was more like an appendectomy than a fish gutting. His nimble fingers did the job rather differently from anything I'd ever seen, and I could gut a fish as well as the next one, and I'd grown up amongst the slickest fish dressers in the world. But Dr. Burgess was the scientist, and he explained that he was working on smelt habits—age, migrations, food, and all such. Years later—I was grown then—his exhaustive studies resulted in a small but comprehensive pamphlet, and I suppose my catch of smelts played some part in the compilation of this definitive work.

Anyway, Dr. Burgess talked on to me about smelts. He put it all down low in language I got. He told about sea-run fish, and how their bodies undergo a biological and chemical change when they get ready to move up into fresh water. I can remember the look in his eyes when he said, "It's a kind of osmosis . . ." He looked at me to see if osmosis meant anything, and of course it didn't. So he told how chemicals will pass through a membrane and equalize each other, and he explained how the cells in the body of a fish work out the salt-water aspect and take on a fresh-water aspect while the fish is working back and forth in the brackish water between fresh and salt, until one day he is able to leave the salt and go up into the brooks about his business.

Dr. Burgess told about the eels—how the European eels never come to our country, and our eels never go to Europe. All on account of this back-handed osmosis, because it takes three years for a European eel to reach the fresh-water stage, but it takes only a year for ours. So if ours go to Europe they get fresh-water ready about half-way over and die. If theirs come here, they start up into the rivers before they're ready, and then they die. Very simple. No mystery about it, really, except that nobody knows why both kinds of eels mate in just about the same place in the ocean.

Only the female eels come up into fresh water, Dr. Burgess said. The next night at the smelt brook I told that to one of the men and he laughed at me. I found out then how hard it is to expound wisdom to the ignorant—a sadness came over me and I was hurt. The trouble was, of course, that I didn't have the weight of importance. The laughter was highest when a quiet voice, that of Dr. Burgess, spoke out of the shadows at the rear of the smelting group, and told the man I was quite right. Dr. Burgess was recognized as an authority, you see, and after that everybody knew that only the female eels came up in the fresh water. I wasn't any more right then than I had been before, but I found out that there are times when being right isn't much help. Dr. Burgess stood in the light of the fire that night and told about eels, and the whole group sat there glued and listened to him, and they forgot all about driving the stream until he stopped and reminded them.

Dr. Burgess always cleaned my smelts after that. And he'd tell about salmon and trout—charr, he said. He spoke about the many kinds of charr, and how the *Salmo Sebago* really got landlocked and was exactly the same fish in his time as the sea-run Atlantic Salmon. The salmon in cans, he said, isn't a salmon at all, but is quite another fish like a salmon. He showed me trout in tanks, and he could take them out of fresh water and put them in salt and back again and they could live in both. He showed me the scales of fish under a microscope, the only way to tell how old a fish is. He said fish keep growing the longer they live, and he didn't know of any other kind of life that did.

It was funny, the way both ends of the range of knowledge came to us boys on these smelting trips. We got the stories around the fire, and learned a lot of new words and expressions, and ended up with pure scientific research. I've never cleaned a fish since that time that I didn't open his stomach and look to see what he'd been eating. One time I got a live tree frog back for my trouble, and he hopped off without a word of thanks.

There's been a lot written about smelting here in Maine in my time, mostly about how good they taste and the right ways to cook them. Somehow, I don't feel a mess of smelts is the *sine qua non* of an excursion to the smelt brook. It's the things you get besides the smelts—the spring moon over the spruces, the rush of the snow-water through the sets, the sudden excruciating breathlessness when you go in over your boots and have a legful of that same water. It's the woodsmoke and the sandwiches, and the fir boughs you've brought in to keep yourself off the wet ground. The flash of that little back line under the gleam of your lantern—a gleam sometimes that the old-sters likened to the glow of a yellow-eye bean. The flash and the tremendous urge that sends it against that icy spring run-off far up into the shallows under the banks for a rendezvous with the whole great future of the universe. It's the feel of that sandpaper hide in your numbed fingers, sandpapered for the spring spawning run because

something about smelts makes it helpful. It's the walk
home through the woods in the dawn with a bag of smelts
over your shoulder—perhaps matching the dawn-age return from the chase with food for the cave. You don't
always know, but smelting in the spring is a part of some
kind of a scheme, because it certainly wasn't a love of fried
smelts that made us all go down to salt water and flirt with
death by exposure. In fact, I never really liked smelts to
eat, and never understood why people rave about them so.
I'd just as soon have pork chops. But it wasn't smelts we
went for, and now that I'm older I can see it wasn't. We
went to be out in the night, satisfying a basic urge to take
food for the taking, to sit by the fire and talk or listen, to
be there close to the difference between salt and fresh
where this "kind of osmosis" takes place.

SOME intellectuals might make a distinction between the hell we raised in my town and the modern matter of juvenile delinquency. Such a distinction could be made, because nobody in our town ever was accused of criminal tendencies, even when we did our worst. Fourth of July was more of an event than Halloween with us. Halloween was a great time for tick-tack-toes, and we had several kinds, not all lethal, but mostly it was a chance for the small ones to gibber in the streets and run about until their pumpkins got smashed. Fourth of July was not optional—we were obliged to celebrate. But not much went on at other times of the year that couldn't be excused as the boy's idea of good, clean fun, and we made amends when amends were necessary, and I don't remember that anybody ever accused us of maladjustment or instability.

Fourth of July always called for a bonfire in the square. This was so much an expected thing that the older folks always turned out for it, and the fire department always mobilized and wet down the buildings of the square. That was in itself a kind of celebration, and before any of us touched a match to the pyre we had the same thing as a nod from the chief that everything was ready. I'd like to know what would happen if anybody set off a bonfire like those in the middle of the square today. The fire department would put it out, for one thing, and then everybody would be looking for somebody to pay for the gates, wagons, blinds, barrels, and whatever else had been collected for the occasion. One year we located a perfectly dandy source for our fuel. The shoe factory had foolishly moved a lot of their racks outdoors so they could do some interior repairing on the building, and had left them unguarded. These racks were a hardwood frame on castors, joined at four tier-levels with half-inch birch dowels. They were used in the factory to pass the shoes, during manufacture, from one department to the next. Each operation was done and the shoes returned to ·the racks afterward. Ultimately the racks arrived at the inspection and packing department, and then they were returned back to the stitching room to be loaded up again. I imagine each rack would hold a hundred pairs of shoes, easily. The beauty of them was that they became coated in time with rubber cement. As boys, we didn't recognize the combustible nature of this chemical compound, but we did see in the racks a definite construction advantage.

For one thing, we could push them up the street on the castors and didn't have to lug them. Then we could pile them steadily one on the other. A good crowd turned out that night, and we trundled all the crates up from the shoe factory and piled them in the square. Somehow, none of the older folks who happened to be around seemed to sense just what these things were. At least nobody raised a hue and cry. After the firemen had everything wet down good Bunny Osgood took a rag soaked in kerosene and went up and touched things off.

The rescue of Bunny was one of the outstanding feats of heroism of my time. It wasn't from the fire we rescued him. When the rubber cement exploded like the third and last call to doom, Bunny backed up about a hundred yards and then struck out for the north country, screaming and yelling. We thought he'd been hurt, and we raced up the street to rescue him. His only trouble was being blinded by the flash, and he couldn't see anything, and he thought we were fire demons trying to hold him. Most of us got bad scratches and bites and kicks from Bunny before we subdued him. If we hadn't rescued him, he'd be going yet.

The fire he'd started shot up into the outer reaches of infinity and caused a kind of group paralysis among the firemen. They didn't know what it was, but instantly the entire business section of the town was threatened by the intense heat. Within minutes a thousand people had assembled, at a respectable distance. The firemen, when they came to, began running around in circles, and everybody was ordering everybody else to do something, and nobody did anything. They had a couple of good gasoline pumper engines in the town then, but the fire so distracted everybody that before anybody thought to get a hoseline going, Chet Bubar and Horace Mawhinney had trotted up to the old hose house, and had come back with the ancient hand tub with its reel of hose. Somehow, in the excitement, this struck everybody as the ultimate in amusing situations, and in no time at all they had the brakes unfolded, and a stream of water coming in reaching squirts, and there was laughing and cheering, and even a song as they strove for the rhythm needed on those old machines.

The fire, however, was so hot they couldn't get near

it, and the efforts with the hand tub calmed down the other firemen so they got their lines set up again, and order prevailed, and from three sides firemen moved in to assault the menace. By this time, however, the rubber cement had exhausted itself, the aged birch dowels had been consumed, and the fire suddenly subsided as if by magic into a red-hot pile of castors. Everybody looked sheepish, and we boys felt the occasion had been handled well. We were already off on another tack, and about all we ever heard from the incident was a remark a few weeks later from one of the shipping clerks in the shoe factory that the new racks were a great improvement, and they should have had new ones long ago. I don't remember any chastisement, but I do believe that each of us boys would have agreed that we'd gone a little too far. Perhaps the thing was merely instruction, after all, and we had to learn our lesson that way.

We always put wagons on the Town House roof, and things like that. We had our cranks who got extra attention. One year every boy in town saved whiskey bottles—picking them out of the dump, or out of trash barrels, or taking one that had been used for turpentine in the shop for years—and on the Fourth of July we had over two thousand to set on the steps and front lawn of the fine old sea-captain house whose mistress was local president of the W. C. T. U. The idea was suggested to us by one of the elders of the village; casually, of course. And most indirectly. The event was considered an overwhelming success by almost everybody. The event itself was nothing compared to the implication in the fact that the boys of our town could find over 2,000 whiskey bottles in the space of a year—particularly since Maine was constitutionally dry in that enigmatic era.

Without the slightest doubt our most successful Fourth of July stunt was the night we tricked the janitor of the Methodist Church into the belfry. He was a devout and pious man, and we should have been ashamed of ourselves, but he was also tactless enough to brag that he would keep the boys from ringing the bell all night. He should have taken a tip from one of the Congregational ministers in town who opened the church every Fourth of July and had sandwiches and cocoa in the vestry, and personally ascended the ladder with any boys who wanted to ring the old rauncher of a bell up there. The result was that we had sandwiches and cocoa, and scarcely rang the bell at all, being more intent on ringing the Methodist, Baptist and Universalist bells because people told us we couldn't.

On this particular year, Jimmie Farwell stayed after prayer meeting Wednesday night, and hid in a closet until Mr. Hunnewell, the janitor, had locked up. Then Jimmie let himself out through the vestry window and thus left the window unlocked. The next day was the one for ringing bells for the Fourth, being the third, and we all went in through that window and went up in the belfry and took the bellrope up through the hole and threw it off over the edge so it went down to the ground. Then we went out, and we saw Mr. Hunnewell come to the church shortly after supper and take up his defense position, in a chair at the foot of the stairs going up in the steeple. When we felt the time was right we went up on the church lawn and tolled a couple of times on the bell—gentle-like, somewhat wistful was the tone. Mr. Hunnewell did what we thought he would do, he rushed up into the belfry, and by that time we'd gone in through the vestry window and taken down the ladder. Mr. Hunnewell thus remained in the belfry while we rang the bell. We had to ring the bell, because the minute we stopped Mr. Hunnewell could have slipped off the rope. As long as we kept it going, he couldn't get near enough without running the risk of losing an arm or being pushed out of the belfry. We worked in shifts, but along in the morning somebody slacked off long enough for Mr. Hunnewell to effect surcease, and he spent the rest of the darkness in quiet. I don't know how he got down, but he was down the time of the next meeting of the trustees, and he resigned. They raised his pay and he reconsidered, but as long as he was janitor we never saw him again on the night before the Fourth.

There wasn't a year went by but what we pulled the cotter pins on Joe Lefebre's horserake. Joe was a great hand to get hot, as the saying was, and after he got hot enough he would rake hay with a pacing mare he had, and it was quite a sight. Joe didn't really do much raking, because he drove at such a clip the windrows came fast, and he tripped so often that the teeth were never down. It got so a number of people assembled to watch this, and one year Pinky Darling and I pulled the pins out and waited to see what might happen. I suppose some folks might think our little stunt had a certain element of homicide in it, but it's well known that nothing much ever happens to a drunk, and on top of that, nothing ever happened to Joe either.

The funny thing about pulling the pins on a horserake seems to be that both wheels always come off at the same time. We expected one wheel to drop off, but it never did. Always both wheels at once. So as Joe was going up the field yelling at his mare and the teeth were clicking in and out of the trip mechanism, the wheels came off and canted just a hair out of line and went off into the woods on each side of the field. Joe continued along in midair for quite a distance, not knowing anything about his wheels, and then the force of gravity gradually took over. The rake teeth dug into the ground and began snapping open and shut, throwing clods of the mea-

dow in all directions, and then the forward motion gradually came to a trot, the trot to a walk, and the walk to
nothing. Joe seemed to think something was amiss. After
he located the 'wheels and put them back he was almost
sober again, and the crowd on hand, which refused to
assist in finding and restoring the wheels, went home. The
thing wasn't much by itself, but it must have been fifteen
full years that we did that annually to Joe.

There must be some dainty distinction between our
boyhood escapades and the present misdeeds of juvenile
delinquents. We had some project going on most of the
time, and none of them was primarily designed to promote
peace and quiet. But we kept out of trouble somehow,
and I guess the only answer is that trouble wasn't so
loosely construed when people were more friendly-like in
the small town, and a boy was supposed to learn right
from wrong by doing some of each. It could be, but I'm
not sure. At least we were never desperate for amusement.

Saunders

THE educational experience we had, as supplied for us by the school board at public expense, seems now to have been mostly a series of declamations. There must be some reason why the Friday afternoon speaking sessions weigh so heavily in the recollection of the time. My own idea is that it was good for us, but a great many brainy people of a later date pooh-pooh the whole thing and say it was a barbarous method of wasting time that should otherwise have been spent in participation parties, learning by doing, and certain other improvements. I can't say that speaking pieces appealed to us at the time, but I do know that when my crowd gets together today we always wind up by laughing at the many funny things that happened on Friday afternoons, and I don't remember that we do much talking about algebra, Wheatstone Bridges, ablative absolutes, or Gresham's Law. Some of my schoolmates appear at times now to have a certain paucity of knowledge, but if you say to them, "There was a time . . ." most of them will finish the *Ode on Intimations* without a flicker. I do not know why this is so.

The final object of the year, in this field, was the tri-town speaking contest, when pupils from the high schools in the near-by towns met us in open competition for prizes of $5, $3, $2 and Honorable Mention. All year we worked up to that point. We had already been speaking since our earliest grades, so there was no need in high school to have the teacher explain to us what he meant when, on about the second day, he announced that speaking would be held on Friday afternoons.

It meant that everybody would have a piece to speak, but that only five or six would be called upon. Nobody knew what order the declamations would take, but before the term was up everybody would have his chance. Once you learned a piece you had only to sit tight until called for, but once you had given yours it was smart to rush out and learn another against the future. So we all brushed up on something, and Friday afternoon there was great excitement to see who would be first.

The pieces for speaking were set by custom. Once in a while somebody would find a new one, but that was unusual. For the most part we operated from *speakers* and anthologies, and they were well worn and ancient. This meant that by the time anybody got through high school he knew them all and everybody else knew as much. Custom prevented any girl from repeating *Regulus to the Carthaginians,* because that was a boy's piece, and no boy ever gave *The Old Violin.* But the girls all knew about *Regulus,* and the boys could have given *The Old Violin.*

One thing I've never understood was the reluctance of the judges and teachers to approve anything humorous. A piece that brought laughter had no chance of winning at all, and was indulged without being accepted. There were a number of monologues adapted from the vaudeville stage that came up regularly, but they never won either marks or prizes. One year I carefully memorized some of *Innocents Abroad* where the smart-aleck tourists were having fun with the Italian guide over Columbus being on a *bust*, and Mark Twain was never any funnier. But the teacher suggested that if I should be chosen for the finals, it would be better if I learned *The Man without a Country* or *A Message to Garcia*. Incidentally, it was *Gar-sha* in them days.

I know now, of course, as Molière said, that it is serious business making people laugh, but the technical side of humor wasn't appreciated back then, and levity was regarded as frivolous. I remember that I was chosen for the finals, and I memorized *The Man without a Country*, and I gave it with profound gravity, and I didn't win anyway. Mother said I should have stuck to the funny one, because it was better to amuse people than it was to win a prize, and the big trouble with a speaking contest was the overpowering depression that came from so much uninterrupted dignity. But Mother and the judges never saw eye to eye.

I am not sure what it was the speaking program taught us. It certainly was not the ability to face an audience and speak. We never learned too well to cover up a lapse in memory. The student who could safely ad lib until he resumed the thread of his discourse was never complimented for that ability. Instead, he was graded down because he forgot. The book was always held on the speaker, and any deviation from the established text was noted adversely. I don't think it was poise and equanimity we learned. As I think back on some of the speaking poses we used, it was evident the teachers weren't too eager to see us in an alert speaker's stance. There was, kicking around somewhere, a story of the boy who couldn't recite until he had thrust his big toe into a knothole in the floor. By worming his toe around in this thought-provoker he was able to spout at any length, and no word was too difficult or any disquisition arduous. He never looked at his audience, nor did his audience ever look at anything except his big toe, which he kept screwing into the hole assiduously. The story goes on that one day a classmate stuck a cork stopper into the hole, and when this young man arose to recite and couldn't find any place to stick his toe, a great heavy silence that you could cut with a knife hung throughout the classroom, and the young man was speechless. The knothole or knot was also used by many other pupils as a focal point for the eyes, and I don't remember that any teacher ever bothered much to tell the hypnotized child that he should elevate his features so people could see him and hear him. Those who spoke were graded solely on the physical endurance necessary to carry through the required time. Voice, diction, articulation, expression, and gestures were left to nature, and nature was never generous.

This, of course, was the classroom fashion. Once a pupil had been selected for the final contest, he had the benefit of coaching. Every town, I suppose, has some woman in it who studied drama once and is recognized as a speaking contest coach. In our town she was really very good, and her success at making poor speakers into good ones was phenomenal. Her remarks about gestures tended to give everybody the same kind of a gesture at precisely the same time. I seem to remember that gestures were known as *movements*, because they included not only sweeps of the hand, but also stepping forward and backing up, leaning from the waist to emphasize, and in dramatic renditions such as Is-this-a-dagger-that-I-see they became extremely emotional and sometimes alarming. There will always be something ludicrous in the sound of a high school soprano effecting the voice characteristics of Othello or Ethan Allen while stepping backward and sweeping the hand. But the gestures won many a contest, even though I remember one winner who made movements representing the slaughter of the innocents when everybody in the hall knew the gestures wouldn't even cope with a black fly.

One year Bennie Adams memorized *The Rime of the Ancient Mariner*. I have tried to tell people that now and then, and they do not believe me. But he did. It was away along in November or so before the teacher came to him, and he arose confidently and strode to the front of the room, where he locked his arms across his chest, fixed his eyes on the picture of Abraham Lincoln at the rear of the room, and began:

"The Rime of the Ancient Mariner, by Samuel Taylor Coleridge. Argument. How a Ship, having crossed the line . . ."

At this point Mr. Besford, our principal, was heard to say, "Oh, Lord God!" and we turned to look at him. He had got up from his desk and gone over to the bookshelf, where he picked down a book and opened to *The Ancient Mariner*. He sat down, and followed Bennie, word for word, and when it was all over he said that Bennie hadn't missed a word. Bennie, however, was only starting his piece when the bell rang and it was time to go home. It took four weeks to get through the thing, and Bennie stopped in the middle of a line if that's where he was when the bell rang, and the next week he would pick up with the very word he stopped on. There was a feeling that Bennie wasn't altogether bright in all respects, and that may have been so, but he's the only person I ever knew who memorized *The Rime of the Ancient Mariner*, and I am glad I knew him.

The greatest crime was to forget a piece. In class, the

teacher could prompt you, but this was not sporting in the contest. You had to be given a chance to recover by yourself, and it was only in the final extremity of mortification that the coach would give you one faint word to start you off again. Sometimes it would be only the first syllable of a word. If you had to have more than that, you might just as well go and sit down, because you couldn't win then anyway. The prize depended mostly on memory.

For whatever such is worth, it is true that memory gives many an older person, today, a certain amount of poetry and literature that more improved methods of teaching do not seem to inculcate. I have friends, who at the slightest encouragement, will stand up and repeat *Spartacus to the Gladiators* word for word, and the whole room full of people will chime in on, "There are no noble men but Romans—let the carrion rot!" Within the week I have heard a grown man, sedate and important in this world's affairs, bring Sheridan all the way from Winchester without missing a word. The spectacle, I assure you, is stimulating. It revives a deep belief in the goodnesses of the olden times. It also makes you feel like getting up and giving *Thanatopsis* to show that you belong to the same fraternity, and before you know it the evening has gone, and you have been a child again, screwing your toe in the knothole, and you have re-heard *Barbara Frietchie, The Dead Ship of Harpswell, Casabianca, Diedrich Knickerbocker's Yankee Farmer's Shingle Palace, The Painter of Seville, Horatius at the Bridge,* and if heaven favors the gathering, *The Death of Benedict Arnold.*

I don't care what the modern specialists say, speaking contests were good for us, and the things we learned from them were very real, even if nobody knows what they were.

I GOT down off a load of hay one summer in a fashion
that I have never recommended to others, and found when
I stood up again that I had broken my arm. This was too
bad, because we still had three more loads to get in, and
it wasn't easy for Mr. Chadburn to find help that would
work as cheaply as I would. Mr. Chadburn always said
the workman was worthy of his hire, and then he would
pay very little. My method of getting down off this load
of hay was to lose my balance and fall off over the side
just as we were going by a stone wall.

When I stood up I could see that my arm was broken.
My hand was upside down, and there was a bump on my
wrist the size of a goose egg, but not quite that color. Mr.
Chadburn looked at it and said that it was broken. I
went home and my father said it was broken. My mother
sat on the steps and began to weep, and I told her it
didn't even hurt me that much, so she smiled a little and
said she guessed we'd both recover. Then they took me
down to see Dr. Prosser and he looked at my arm and

wiggled my fingers and confirmed our diagnoses. He said, "Take him home and I'll be right up. Get Dr. Pillsbury, I'll need him." And that was when Dr. Pillsbury came into my life on a professional basis. Dr. Prosser had been in it before, because we "took from him" as the saying went, and he was recognized all over the state as one of the best medical men and surgeons to be had. Our town was lucky to have him. Kept up, he did, and wasn't really a small-town doctor at all. He used to take our people into some of the big hospitals and do the operating himself. Other doctors who were specialists in the cities would come for miles to watch him. He wrote things for medical publications, and was always engaged in some important professional discussion. Ahead of his time in a lot of things. He almost got run out of town once because he refused to fumigate schoolhouses. Every old woman knew that you had to fumigate schoolhouses. But Dr. Prosser said, "Do as much good to burn a tallow candle," and he wouldn't fumigate. He wrote a piece about that, afterward, for a magazine. He had another fight once with Aaron Yeakson over a mustard plaster. Aaron thought they were good, but Dr. Prosser told him he might just as well stick them on a pine stump, for all the good they did. Aaron told all around about it, and folks were divided for a long time.

But as I look back now, I can see that Dr. Prosser actually knew altogether too much. He was too good a doctor. And there must have been something he lacked, because it was Dr. Pillsbury who had the fuller life, and the greater esteem, and I suppose a bigger practice—because he took care of a lot of people that other doctors wouldn't agree were sick. And Dr. Pillsbury was never accounted an exceptionally fine physician when experts gathered and discussed great achievements. But Dr. Pillsbury satisfied all the requirements of the small-town doctor, and although he did keep up to date in many ways, he would always approve a mustard plaster if you thought a mustard plaster was what you needed, and he would fumigate clear out into the back woodlot if you asked him to. And I have arrived, therefore, at a conclusion, which is that some doctors treat patients, and some doctors treat people. If I were to criticize the great field of modern medicine, it would be to say that people are no longer people when they become sick and apply to a physician. Psychiatry, as an upstart profession, probably has an advantage in this respect, although my claim is that the country doctor had his own proper balance in these two fields and with his limited facilities he knew more than both of them. Because he knew when to put on mustard plasters and when to refrain. Anyway, my father got Dr. Pillsbury to come up, and Dr. Pillsbury etherized me to the complete satisfaction of Dr. Prosser, and Dr. Prosser put my arm back so you'd never know it was broken.

Dr. Pillsbury was better than six feet tall, and had no more girth than a moonbeam. He wore a beard because beards had been regular equipment when he was just out of medical school. For over 50 years he had practiced medicine in our town, and he had seen a lot of things happen. The wisdom in his head must have taxed his cells and membranes, because he was one of these rare people who know something about everything to some degree. He did something I have never known another doctor of medicine to do—he went to a veterinarian college long enough to pick up some pointers on animal troubles. So he could help the farmers. Everywhere he went to take care of somebody, there would be a dog or a cow in distress, and he wanted to be able to help. Our local vets always seemed to take to drink just prior to an emergency call, but I can't say they were very often much help. But Dr. Pillsbury was perfectly willing to sew up a barbwire gash or make a hound dog comfortable, and that is a fine thing. Most doctors feel animals are beneath their dignity, which is a kind of ignorance and should be corrected by proper instruction in colleges of medicine. A dog can be wept for, too. And I have seen farmers whose economy and happiness were a good deal more wrapped up in their cows than their wives. Not too many, but some. A doctor should know these things, and Dr. Pillsbury did.

His office was little more than a study. There were no murderous looking cases of instruments about. He had a library of medical books, but he also had some law books, and along with these the classics and anything else that appealed to him. He was always reading when somebody came in. And sometimes he would read you a little of it before he put the book down—depending on the occasion. I wouldn't wonder if sometimes some patients forgot what they came for before he decided to look at their tongues. There was nothing swift about him, ever. He never made a snap judgment; he never rushed. But he had a steady gait. If he was called, and you lived in the village, he would take his little bag and walk to your house. If you lived out in the country, he hitched up his driving mare and rode out. He had a stick on the wheel, and every time it clicked it meant so many feet, and he knew the exact distance to every doorstep in town. They said as a young man when he first put a stick on his buggy, he got engrossed one day and rode along counting clicks until he was three miles beyond the place where the woman was having a baby.

When he got back the husband was waiting in the road, and the husband shouted, "Half price this time, Doc, the child is born!" And when the man paid, Dr. Pillsbury would only take half his amount. I don't want to identify that lad too closely, but he grew up and lived and died and was always known as Half-Price Dick. Another time, when he was just beginning to practice, a farmer came for him on a baby case, and Dr. Pillsbury rode out in a driving blizzard to find that the call was previous by about six hours. Because of the storm he thought he'd better stay, so he sat down to wait, and the only reading matter in the house was a Bible and a book on shorthand. So Dr. Pillsbury learned shorthand that afternoon, and found it useful many times. The Bible, he could quote backwards anyway.

One evening in the drugstore, while he was waiting for some medicine to be put up, he entertained a group of six or so, I was one of them, by discussing home remedies, and I think his attitude shows much of his knowledge and judgment. It was from him, actually, that I first learned that lanolin is woolgrease. In recent years a soap manufacturer has been doing a big business advertising a hair shampoo with lanolin in it. I have wondered if he would sell as much if he advertised that it contained woolgrease. As a basis for salves, lanolin was used long ago by country people who had no scientific way of arriving at its soothing and healing nature. Possibly they noticed that a torn sheep heals quickly. Dr. Pillsbury used lanolin as an example of the kind of homespun treatment that somehow hits on a pure scientific truth, and he explained that he wasn't inclined to scoff at old wives' treatments as much as some.

He told about a woman who had erysipelas, and he wasn't doing too well treating it. The old grandma in the home told him she could do better, so they divided up the patient and each took a side. In a few days the grandma had done a better job. Her treatment was crushed cranberries, and Dr. Pillsbury studied up on it until he found that the acid in cranberries was the same acid used in a routine erysipelas salve. He guessed that it was concentrated more in cranberries, and so the cranberries bleached when the salve wouldn't. But the point Dr. Pillsbury made was to raise the question of how that grandma knew about crushed cranberries. The home remedy was far from a joke. "I've used cranberries myself, since," he said. He refused to laugh at a piece of salt pork tied over a wound to "draw out the poison." The idea has gone around since, I understand, that salt pork is sometimes as unclean as the wound itself, but Dr. Pillsbury seemed to think the remedy had saved a good many people from blood poisoning, and he wasn't averse to it if it worked. "That's the trouble," he said, "the minute you start ridiculing these things, you run into somebody who finds they work, and if you look into it, you find that they do. No matter how many big doctors pooh-pooh the idea of salt pork, if it takes out poison, it's worth using. I'm not so much interested in the philosophies and theories as I am in getting the poison out, and I doubt if the patient is."

But Dr. Pillsbury was circumspect enough to discredit fish drafts for fever. Some of our coastal people believed that a salt fish, preferably a cod, strapped to the bottom of the patient's feet would draw out a fever and leave the sick man cool and improved. Dr. Pillsbury said that was going a little too far, except that it gave somebody something to do, and somebody with nothing to do around a sick room can sometimes be a nuisance.

"In other words, they're good too," said Perley Curtis, one of the group in the drugstore.

"Why yes, in a manner of speaking, yes. Very little, in medicine, is wholly useless."

He told of a "corn sweat." He said out in the corn country you could boil the long ears of dry corn, and when they were red hot lay them about a patient under blankets. Under his arms, between his legs, along his body. "And he'll sweat," said Dr. Pillsbury.

ट॰ 2 2 8

"Sh'd think he would," said Perley. "I know I would. Maybe you'd get the same effect if you used steam-clams."

Dr. Pillsbury said it was an idea, and if pressed for a needed sweat without other means, he would be the first to try steamed clams.

Asbury Thomas said, "That time I had the congestion, seemed to me I was hot enough to steam some clams, myself."

Dr. Pillsbury said, "One of my great desires in this world is to see you sometime when you aren't hot enough to steam clams."

"Well," As said, "if I stay cooled off any length of time, you want to come right over, because if I ain't dead I'll be dying, and if anybody dies around here without you in on it, it won't seem right, somehow."

"You are maligning my whole profession to such an extent I shall look forward eagerly to your demise, As," said Dr. Pillsbury, and there was a lot more of the same before they got back to home remedies. Dr. Pillsbury was always getting mixed up in these seemingly hostile fencing matches, and was usually credited with a demolishing parting shot that would get quoted around for weeks. His advantage lay in his intimate knowledge of everybody, and that included their touchy subjects. There wasn't much he didn't know, and the town had few people he couldn't prescribe for with his eyes shut.

Along in there one year we had a blizzard that tied up the railroad and brought two or three ocean liners into our harbor for haven, and just as it struck Dr. Pillsbury had started out for the Melvin house on the upper road. Mrs. Melvin was expecting. Mr. Melvin had driven in after the doctor, because telephones were still mostly a village matter, and he hurried right back home again while Dr. Pillsbury was getting ready. Well, after waiting a time, Mr. Melvin thought it was funny the doctor didn't come, and Mrs. Melvin was expecting a good deal harder now, so Mr. Melvin hitched up his horse again and went back to town. Where or how he met and passed Dr. Pillsbury on the way has never been known, but he did, and he got to town to alarm everybody with the news that Dr. Pillsbury was lost in the storm. He felt Mrs. Melvin needed the doctor, so Mr. Melvin urged the organization of a posse to set out and search. Dr. Pillsbury, meantime, had got out to the Melvin farm without any trouble, had stabled his horse, and had delivered Mrs. Melvin of twins, one of each, and everything was fine and dandy, if not hunky-dory. Then, upon observing the violence of the storm, he decided to spend the night. He went out and fed his horse, brought in wood for the parlor stove, and after Mrs. Melvin had dozed a little he introduced her babies to her, talked a while, got some supper started, and was doing all right.

In the village, a posse had been rounded up, but because the storm had shut down and a howling wind had sprung up, the men decided it would be wiser to wait until morning. So they agreed to wait until daybreak, and they convinced Mr. Melvin that his wife would accommodate herself to the situation through latent female powers, and it was better for her to have her husband alive the next day than to have him freeze to death tonight. Mrs. Pillsbury gave him two little white pills and he went to sleep. Roads were obliterated in that storm, and some of them weren't found until spring—and keeping Mr. Melvin in town was wise.

Well, the next morning they were just starting out on snowshoes to find Dr. Pillsbury when Dr. Pillsbury walked into town with Mr. Melvin's old bearpaw snowshoes and showed great surprise at seeing so many men up so early in the morning. "Something the trouble?" he asked, and the men all looked at him, and then looked at each other, and they said, "No, nothing at all." So Mr. Melvin walked out home and found his wife comfortable and fed, and proud, and also found the breakfast dishes washed and the bed made and the woodbox filled.

Beyond any possible shadow of a doubt, Dr. Pillsbury was as fine an obstetrician as ever lived, and for very good reasons. First, he had had so many babies. And then, he had them in so many widely differing places under so many varied conditions. Few of the conditions would be termed ideal. The rushing of a woman to a hospital had yet to be thought up, and was never done unless serious complications were forecast. In those cases, Dr. Pillsbury left the job with the hospital. His babies were born at random, sort of, and he used to say the only place he never delivered a baby was on a moving flatcar, but he expected to any minute now. His ability to make shift was probably no different from that of any country doctor in a thousand other places, and may not have been as good as some, but like the others, he had to do it. He did all the storied things—appendectomies on kitchen tables, and many an operation while somebody held a lamp and somebody else held the patient.

In Dr. Pillsbury's time most people died of heart failure and old age. These causes were entered officially in the public records. Medicine has become more explicit, although Dr. Pillsbury might point out that death was just as effective when it was less precisely defined. Dr. Pillsbury figured if a patient was in his 90's and died, it was silly to worry over causes. Old age was cause enough. It always struck me that Dr. Pillsbury's own demise, which came when he was 94, was unnecessarily classified as coronary thrombosis by the recently arrived young physician who had been called. If the new doctor had known his patient, he'd have put down "Old Age and Fullness of Life."

ૐ 2 3 1

Dr. Pillsbury was a philosopher first. He actually quoted Aristotle in Town Meeting. Some people couldn't have done it, but he did, and everybody listened. They may not have known Aristotle, but they knew the doctor. He applied the humanities to about everything he did. And if something came up in any field that was new, he found out about it and reported back in due time. And he could play upon the people in our town as if they were a piano. Once he came to see Dan Thurlow, who was one of these hearty people who never had a sick day, and consequently was scared silly when he got took down. He really was sick, as it turned out, but Dr. Pillsbury wasn't going to admit it while the man's fears were the strongest. So when the doctor came into the sick room he saw a newspaper on the bed, and he said, "Oh, the paper—I haven't seen a paper in two days," and he sat down by the window and began to read it.

"But Doc," Dan said, "I'm sick."

"Yes, I been notified. You'll get well."

"But dammit, Doc, don't just sit there and read that paper, I feel awful."

"You may feel worse before you're better."

"I feel like I was dying."

"This paper prints the silliest editorials. Here's one here trying to figure out how Europe feels. What does an editor in Portland know about Europe? Why don't he write about things here in Maine, things he has a fair chance to know about? I think I'll write him a letter and say so."

"For God's sake, Doc Pillsbury, will you put that damn paper down and give me a pill, or something?"

"I suppose that is what I came for, after all. What seems to be the trouble, now? Something sore?"

"I just feel awful. I think I may die."

"Well, what of it. People do. Don't mean a thing to

anybody else. If you die, you'll be surprised how soon the general grief will pass away. It won't bother you any, either. So what of it? You may get well, too. People do that. I had a man get well once, and people were going to sue me because I let him. Been eating something you shouldn't, like green corn or scallops?"

Dan got well, and he used to tell all around about the conversation he had that morning. "Damned old coot knew just what he was doing, too—got me so mad I forgot how sick I was, and first thing I knew I felt better. I could have killed him, though. I found out afterward he'd seen that same paper in at least ten other bedrooms, and took it at home himself, besides."

Dr. Pillsbury had one honorary preferment in our town. He was always the recipient of an invitation to the high school graduation—not from any individual, but from the class. Most of us were his babies, and the thing had become a tradition. Tickets were always at a premium, because the church was small, and after the lower classes and parents were seated, with the school board and the selectmen and the ministers in their special pews, there wasn't much room for the general public. Each graduating student would have maybe two tickets to throw around as he pleased, but scarcely ever any more than that unless the class was a small one. But Dr. Pillsbury always got an invitation and had his seat saved for him. Once in a while some thoughtless woman would be having a baby at that time, and some years he'd get called out after he came, but usually he was present and stayed to see what his children did. I guess a lot of the valedictorians actually turned and spoke directly at him, because there were families in our town that thought he was greater than God, and a good deal more available during perplexities.

When Dr. Pillsbury died his daughter burned his account books. Nobody knew, but everybody supposed that his debtors were many. He never sent out a bill in his life. If you paid him, you got no receipt. You could be sick for nothing, in my town, if you wanted to take advantage of Dr. Pillsbury's errant financial arrangements. But people didn't take advantage if they could pay. My mother used to say, "Always pay the doctor—you may need him again and you don't know when it'll be." And I think most people felt the same way. A common sight around our town was seeing somebody stop Dr. Pillsbury on the street and give him some money. The doctor would fold it, run it down in his pants pocket, and stand and talk. And if you didn't pay him—well, he always came when you needed him anyway. Dr. Pillsbury was still going strong by the time I left home. He was old, and he didn't go out any more nights. But if you could wait until morning he'd walk over and see what he could do. The other doctors were better doctors, of course, but the truth is that they were a lot less pleasant company. He knew it as well as anybody did. He would probably have contributed some healthy ideas to modern medicine if anybody had asked him to, but it wouldn't have done any good. The smart new men would have said, "What does he know about medicine?" And they would have been right. But I guess Dr. Pillsbury knew so much about human nature that he was able to fool our town a whole lifetime with very little medicine. He certainly knew plenty about our townspeople, and there weren't many of them that didn't turn out to his funeral. It was pretty hard to believe that the old fellow had gone. But of course he has gone, not from my town alone, but pretty much from all towns. And we probably miss him more than we know.

ONE of our high school class rides was a wonderful thing, and required three hayracks with three teams and too many chaperons. The Junior Ride was supposed to be the best, although I had my most fun on our Freshman Ride, and when you came right down to it there wasn't much difference in any of them. The hayracks, loaded with hay into which the riders could snuggle with considerable safe promiscuity, simply carted us out to some predetermined picnic spot, after which they carted us back home again—and all in the nighttime.

The unrivaled success of my Freshman Ride was due to a complete accident, in that I had the loveliest girl in the whole school for my partner, and I wish to speak of it now to show that I, too, had my moments. This girl was a senior, but she was a couple of years older than the class average, on account of having been sickly. She was kept out of school. When she came back she was most determined to keep up with her studies, and wasn't too much given to joining in the play. Her serious attitude made her seem inaccessible when it came to a class ride, although her physical appearance made her more than desirable. She was a strawberry blonde and wore long curls, and maturity had come to her over and above the usual high school amount. She had charm and grace and all those things. It struck me all at once, one day, that nobody would be likely to ask her to go on the class ride, and that this was tantamount to a shame.

My decision to ask her myself was audacity of the worst kind. If she had two years advantage on her class—then my class had a year on me, because I had been unusually astute back in grammar school and had skipped a grade. It was a matter of seven years, at least. So I asked the young woman, one recess, if she would go on the class ride with me, and she acted as if she had been waiting for me to ask her and said yes. I probably missed it completely at the time—but what an opportunity that was to observe the latent female ability at duplicity and deceit! She looked as if she would be overjoyed at my company, and seemed to be thrilled to pieces. And I thought she was. It's only the realizing of later years that tells me she simulated that abundance of delight. And also, I found out later that all the time she was engaged to be married to a man who ran a grocery store in Bangor, and the wedding was to be in June right after graduation. Not only that, but he knew she went on the class ride with me, which was a sad discovery when I made it.

But she went, and we had the most wonderful time. The boys chipped in and paid for the hayracks and teams and the drivers' time, but the girls put up the refreshments. When I called in my short pants, because we didn't go into long pants in those days until we were ready for them, I found my girl had packed a lunch I could hardly lift. We actually had a pie that was still warm when we cut it, and it was the only whole pie I ever heard of on a class ride. We snuggled down in the hay, and the hayracks started out, and into the night we rode singing and laughing, and having fun. There was something fine about squiring this young woman on that ride, and I wasn't hurt when I found my own classmates felt I had overstepped the true bounds of age. Particularly the girls. They resented it. It seemed to me at the time that this didn't make any great amount of difference, because those who didn't envy me my girl would certainly envy me that pie.

The class ride progressed away from town until it arrived at the place the committee had selected for the picnic. Firewood had been gathered, a spring cleaned out, and everything was ready for us to feed up. The teamsters would feed the horses. The teachers and chaperons would make great to-do over preserving the morals of everybody present, a to-do that was successful at all times, as far as I know, except for the year when a former student came home from college and went on a class ride with an English teacher who turned out to be glad he came. The English teacher was supposed to be a chaperon, and her disappearance for the remainder of the occasion caused some talk for a time. After the picnic, we'd load back into the racks, and snuggle down again, and the ride back to town was usually quieter, and it wasn't unheard of for the couples to fall asleep in each other's arms and dream that the ride went on and on and never did get back to the streetlights again. But it always did, and then we had to walk our partners home, and a class ride seemed like a very fine idea.

While most class rides went off as advertised, and little happened to make one different from another, now and then an exception set in. One year some of us in the second hayrack thought we'd like to run up ahead and visit in the first hayrack for a mile or so and see if we couldn't stir up something. So we clambered over the side of the rack and hung by our hands and dropped to the road and ran on ahead. With us was Nell Bryant, who was a tomboy anyway, and when she dropped to the road she chose a very bad place. The rack was just then going over a bridge, and Nell dropped about twenty feet into a deep pool of water. The wheels made so much noise on the wooden bridge that people in the rack didn't hear her elongated scream, but we boys on the road did, and we fished her out. There was a joyously strange happenstance in that—it amused us that a dozen boys could leap down to the road and the bridge would come along just for the one girl. We made more of it than Nell seemed to think was justified. During the picnic, when we steamed clams and roasted frankfurts, Nell hid under a blanket and we turned her clothes on sticks so she'd be dry for the trip home.

Then one class ride we had a teamster who brought a jug of cider with him. He had it tucked under the hay, and nobody knew he was sucking on it until he had taken enough to become generous, and when we were about halfway to the picnic spot enough generosity had been engendered so he turned to our lead chaperon and said, thickly, "Would you take a snort?"

Our lead chaperon was unfamiliar with this expression, so she turned from the roundelay in which she had been assisting and said, "What was that, Mr. Palmer, I didn't hear you?"

"I said, would you take a snort?"

She said, "I don't seem to understand—a snort? A snort of what?"

Palmer said, "A snort of apple juice."

"Apple juice? Gracious, I think that would be nice."

So there was a certain amount of fumbling around in the dark, and then Mr. Palmer said, "Suck on it, pull towards you—you don't play a jug like a floot," and then there was a choke and a cough, and the ringing accusation, "That's cider!"

"Yes, Ma'am," said Palmer. "It's cider."

The chaperons then spread the word that we were in the hands of a raving Phaethon, and while the chaperons worried, we youngsters thought that was fine, and Palmer studied his jug. After a lesson he would touch up the team and we would gallop wondrously for a half mile or so. Then Palmer would haul up and wait for the racks behind, and while he was awaiting he would translate another passage or two. When we got to the picnic spot the chaperons tried to find his jug, but he knew about chaperons himself, and he carried it with him when he fed his horses, and prepared for the trip home. The chaperons, naturally, refused to ride back with him, and instructed us not to ride with him either, so we started out with the whole crowd in two racks, and the happy Mr. Palmer, solo, in the lead. Shortly, however, most of us were able to sneak out of the chaperoned vehicles, and by running fast we caught Mr. Palmer, and when we got to town almost all the boys and girls were in the Palmer rack enjoying the undisciplined environment. Mr. Palmer had reached the conclusion that he was the finest, most intelligent, happiest man in the world by that time, and it's possible he was. My father, when he heard of it, said, "Palmer drunk is ten men sober with horses around." But Mother said she imagined he wouldn't be asked to drive on a class ride again. He wasn't, but I've heard that he didn't care.

Some of these class rides came in the winter on snow, and the screech of logging sleds on packed snow, under a full moon, is something to have in your memory. We liked to picnic at a rural school, or at some farmhouse, then, but there were times when we had our bonfire in the open and made a picnic as if it were summer. But the winter rides were not too frequent, because it was better to spend the time with the bobsleds on Keelhaul Hill. And speaking of rides, there was one. Keelhaul Hill was a mile and a half long on both sides of the valley, and it had some good curves to it. A bobsled to us was a long plank fitted with traverse runners that were made at home. At least a dozen could ride at once, and a dozen is nothing to some of the crowds we had aboard. Planks have been known to snap. And sometimes we really got hurt when the helmsman wasn't too proficient. But the road was ours. In those days the snow wasn't scraped off to reveal the Mother Earth so motorists could bowl along without chains. Teaming was done, and people had sleighs and pungs, and the snow was left where it fell for the general good. The road-breaking equipment was a team of horses or oxen on a front logging sled with a timber stuck across between the runners. The snow was flattened out and packed down, but hardly any of it was pushed off the road. In a day or so enough horses and runners had gone by so the sledding was good. The biggest hazard to bobsledding was the presence of horse manure, and that could sometimes upset a sled. But the runners gradually packed even that down, and a good helmsman would keep clear of the hazard. Another thing, nobody sanded the roads then. If anybody had sanded a road he'd have been lynched. If the teamsters hadn't got him, certainly he'd never have survived the wrath of the bobsledding crowd. In later years I have tried to revive this sport. I've tried to show my children how it was. And the road crews have always beaten me to it, and the hill I select is already sanded to a golden brown, and the snow all pushed out into the ditches, and while we stand there and curse the marvels of modern times, automobiles race by and leer at us. I am sad and there is no joy in me. Even Keelhaul Hill is safe, with all its curves, to high speed motor travel on the worst winter night.

People who had automobiles back in that day either put them up for the winter, or knew enough to stay off sliding hills. The farmers who traveled the road on those good winter coasting nights kept an ear out for an approaching bobsled, and when they heard us screeching and squealing toward them on Keelhaul Hill, they would drive their sleighs out into the snowbank, and they would stay there until they were sure all the sleds out that night had gone down by them. In those days, if you wish to phrase it so, childhood had a right-of-way, and a bobsled was nothing to monkey with. I guess today if anybody tried to slide there he would find a difference prevails. That is too bad. But we did, sometimes, have our picnics on these bobsled evenings, and I think most of us preferred that kind of an evening to a winter class ride.

We preferred it even though sometimes halfway down we'd pile into the ditch and bang ourselves up fearfully. And we'd bang up the sleds, too. We'd all come walking home carrying parts, and then somebody's father or uncle would have to touch up the stove in the shop and put things together again for the next night—because the moon is big for only a few days together during the Maine winter months, and much needs to be done in a short time. We'd notice, one night, that the moon had a ring around it, and then it would cover in, and the next morning snow would be drifting down, and we'd have no more good sliding until the big logging sleds had smoothed out the road. And sometimes not until the coming moon came again— because it wasn't so much fun on dark nights when you couldn't see ahead. And besides, the way Keelhaul Hill went, we never got above two slides an evening—once on each slope. Then we walked back, and the evening had gone and bedtime was with us.

So we had our rides, and what they amounted to is something I guess boys today wouldn't understand. Mother used to say, "You can't ever go back. Things you do now won't ever be done again. You've got to do it now."

Then there's the story of Orville Linscott and his owl,
but I may not be able to show just how it helped me become a man. Orville was a tidy old fellow, and had a
whitewashed little farm at the water's edge. One day he
was rummaging around the shore and he found a duck's
nest. He didn't see what kind of a duck it was when she
took off, but he brought the eggs home in his hat and put
them under a hot hen, and in two or three days they
hatched out. A hen, ordinarily, takes 28 days on ducks
eggs, and because that is quite a stretch for a hen it sometimes takes two hens to go the whole distance. But this
was a lucky hen, because the duck had done most of the
work, and there she was with a clutch of little ones when
she'd hardly more than got started.

They turned out to be mallards. Not many years ago
I heard one of the high-powered naturalists in our fish and
game department make a speech, and he said the mallard

duck never nested in Maine. I tried to tell him the statement had some degree of error in it, because Orville Linscott once had mallard ducks, but he pish-toshed the whole idea and indicated I didn't know what I was talking about. I think I did, all the same, and one of my early achievements was exhibiting domesticated wild mallards in a poultry show—I was the first person ever to do so. Orville gave me a pair of the ducks from that hatching of eggs, and I raised them and exhibited them and saw them produce young, and then I picked them and ate them, and they were mallards. The mallard drake is the most beautiful of all birds, and when I put them in the poultry show the judge went to the superintendent's office and asked what he was supposed to do. He said they had never been shown before, and there was nothing to go by in The American Standard of Perfection, and as far as he could see there was no point in trying to judge them. I won all the prizes.

But before Orville gave me my pair of ducks, he went down in the field and built a pen to keep his ducks in. It was a very neat pen, with peeled tamarack posts, and six-foot chicken wire tacked tightly, and a board running around the ground so nothing could push up the wire and get under. Foxes and cats and dogs like ducks, too. Orville was most proud of his ducks, and asked everybody to come and see them, and during their change from down to feathers he promised me a pair so I could grow some of my own another year. He had no trouble with them at all, and every one of them lived, and after a while they were big enough so he took the hen away. They stopped peeping shortly and took on a fine quack. The female has a loud, but fairly flat quack, much more pleasing to the ear than that of any other duck I ever heard. The mallard male doesn't quite quack, but almost does, and sounds as if he had laryngitis. There were three males and eight females when Orville could tell one from the other. It was a beautiful flock of ducks, and everybody much admired them.

Thinking it over later, I don't know why Orville's ducks should have attracted so much attention. The mallard was very common in those days along the Atlantic flyway, and we had all taken them in the fall and spring along the shore. Live decoys were permitted then, and a lot of people had used mallards. But somehow Orville's affair with his clutch of eggs won popular interest, and we watched the ducks grow as if none of us had ever seen a wild mallard before. So they grew, and along in late summer he gave me my pair, and I took them home and put them in a pen in the henhouse and proceeded to lavish every care upon them. They were as tame as kittens, and ate from my hand, and showed no evidence whatever of having come from wild parents who coursed that strange route along our ocean. So much for that.

But Orville, when fall came, went out one morning to strew corn and talk to his nine mallard ducks, and when he opened the gate and went in he found that he had thirty-three ducks. All but nine of them were flying against the wire fence and acting crazy, and the nine were trotting around the ground and quacking gently and acting very much surprised. The answer was simple. During the night a flock of mallards had cut across the sky on their way south, and they had been saluted by Orville's nine with such enticing hospitality that they came down to see what was going on, and ate up all the mash and had a nice visit. When dawn came they presumably tried to depart, following their seasonal urge, but didn't have runway enough to take off. All they could do was fly against the fence. Orville thought this was a good idea.

The first thing he did was toss some corn to his nine tame ducks, and when they came to feed he picked them up one at a time and slipped celluloid bands on their legs.

Having thus identified his tollers, he spent the rest of the day chasing and picking down his wild ones. He carried them two at a time to his barn, and stabled them in an empty box stall where he could give them attention later. In effect, he set his trap again. The next morning he had a couple dozen or so more, with a few black ducks mixed in, and from then until cold weather he did a good business catching wild ducks. He skun some of them out and passed them around to townsfolk, including us, and some of them he sold on the hoof, and some of them he paired off and made comfortable in various parts of his barn, shed, fish house, and henhouse. It had occurred to him previously that he might make a penny breeding and raising tollers, and that many a duck hunter would be glad to pay for a pair, or maybe three, so they could set out at anchor and quack at wild birds. Such was the custom. You usually put two females, with weighted straps on their legs, on one side of your duck blind, and tethered the male off on the other side. Separating them caused them to quack whenever wild ducks flew over, because the male thought his hens might be molested, and his hens thought they might not. Orville had this all figured out, and was in fine spirits.

The next spring when the nesting season came, Orville trapped some more in his wire, and then he began fixing up all manner of little pens around for the ducklings when they should hatch, and he was definitely in the duck business in a big way. But he came to our house one morning with a sad look in his eye, and told my father that something, or somebody, was stealing his ducks. During the night he would hear a great quacking, and he would rush out thinking somebody was breaking into the pens, and he wouldn't find anything wrong. But each night he was losing some ducks, and the thing was mysterious. My father, who had spent more time on the farm than Orville had, said he guessed he knew what the trouble was, and that he would take a hand. So Orville went home, and that evening my father and I walked over to his place and stuck a tall pole up in the middle of the field, and set a steel trap on top of it. That was the way we always caught owls and hawks around a hen pen, and I suspicioned what was going forward. Then we went home. And the next morning before breakfast Orville came bursting in with the news that we'd caught an owl as big as a bull, and that he was sitting on the pole snapping his beak at a great rate, and a dead duck lay at the foot of the pole. So we went over.

Orville had already decided he would like to keep the owl, because he was a big one, so he had built a wire cage for him. He certainly was a big one. I have never seen a bigger. He could screw his head around a dozen times, and I walked around the pole until I was dizzy to see if he'd wring his own neck. Orville brought a piece of sail cloth, and my father pulled the pole up out of the ground and laid it down. The owl jumped up and down, and clicked his teeth, and hollered a little, and then my father and Orville laid the cloth over him. Then the cloth would jump up and down, and the two of them tried to get the owl settled in one place and held at bay so they could get the trap off.

It took a little while to do, because the owl wasn't helping them very much. My father reached under and released the trap and got his thumb stuck in it and spoke a short piece, and then they carried the owl all bundled up to the new cage and tossed him in, cloth and all. The owl had been caught by one of his toes, and it hadn't hurt him a bit. His talon, being horn, was probably tougher than the trap. He backed up into a neutral corner and snapped his beak and blinked, and made out he was awful mad. Orville reached through the door of the cage, open only a crack, and yanked the cloth out with a nail on the end of a stick, and during the forenoon I rounded up the gang and we all inspected the owl and saw that he was good. Within the next few days everybody in town inspected him, and Orville basked in a kind of glory. He certainly was a magnificent owl.

But the fun was just starting. Owls have to eat. And we learned that owls have a strange manner of taking nourishment. It consists of eating their prey entire, and then regurgitating what they don't care to keep. They don't do this every day, but only when they feel like it. It developed in a week or so that Orville's owl was partial to dead hens. Except in skunking time, when dead hens served to bait a trap, that, was easy, and our little community was glad to find something to do with dead hens. It is strange that so few things have been found to do with them, because everybody has a dead hen now and then, and any way of turning them to profit would be popular. During the next few days Orville accumulated quite a good sized pile of dead hens, one of which the owl ate and regurgitated and was satisfied. Orville put the rest in his wheelbarrow, pushed them out back of the barn, and entombed them under his blackberry bushes.

The thing was pernicious from the start. Orville was in no position to decline accepting these donations, because death to a hen is unpredictable, and there was never any definite time schedule when defunct poultry might be expected. The owl ate when he'd a mind to, and a stockpile of hens was something of an asset. About that time almost anyone else would have called quits, but Orville had taken a fancy to his owl, and was willing to bury hens five days a week to have one good dead one over the week end. Whenever roup or pip struck some luckless flock and wiped out hens like flies, the bereaved owner would load the carcasses on his cart and take them over to Orville, and Orville would convey his thanks and bespeak his gratitude, and then take them out and bury them. Choice was exercised, and Orville's owl got only the finest and very best of dead hens. None that had lingered and wasted made the grade, and the owl ate only those that had been stricken suddenly in their prime.

About this time some nature lover in town pointed out that owls were great eaters of rats, mice and snakes, and that a steady diet of poultry might undermine this owl's constitution and lend him susceptible to the gout, or something worse. So mice were emptied from household traps, and carried to Orville in strawberry boxes, and rats as big as raccoons were taken over on the end of a flat stick, and we observed the owl was not averse to the change. It was but a step, then, to a purely scientific study to find out which things an owl would eat, and which things he wouldn't. When fall came the supply of dead hens fell off, but we did have skunk carcasses. These were politely dissected so no undue disturbance would be caused, although this was purely a hypothetical conde-scension, because by that time the owl's cage smelled worse than any skunk, or combination of skunks, ever did. In fact, comment had given way to complaints, and Orville was asked to move his owl off the lawn and back toward the shore, preferably to the other side of the grove. Or-ville didn't do that, although he did build a bigger cage and shift the owl to a clean site, after which he burned the old cage, and the lavender smoke hung like a pall over the town for a week and made people wish they were dead.

The new cage grew ripe shortly, and except in cold weather was annoying to folks in that end of town. The owl never showed any signs of becoming tame, and not even Orville could safely open the door without being rushed at with much clicking and snapping. Orville made a small hinged trap on the side of the cage, through which

he could extract some of the more objectionable super-
fluities with a hoe, but the habits of an owl are deep-seated,
and lessons in neatness were ignored. On a down wind
there was no limit to the discomfort of villagers, and even
against a stiff breeze the owl was able to make his presence
known for quite a distance. Mrs. Stevens got up a petition,
but not many signed it. We knew Orville pretty well, and
we also knew Mrs. Stevens.

But in time even Orville got enough of it. I would
guess he had the owl ten years, altogether, not any less
than that certainly. The donation of departed derelicts
continued all that time, and Orville could raise buckwheat
a fathom high on any part of his surplus cemetery. He had
one of the richest farms in Maine. And the vilest smelling
in the country. And after about that length of time he
began to talk about getting rid of the owl. "I guess I
better get rid of him," he'd say, partly to see what people
said, at first, and partly to nurture his courage. He liked
the owl. Why, I don't know, but he did. So one day he
made a crate and put the owl in it, and sent it by express
to the zoo at Franklin Park, in Boston.

The town was delighted. The big cage was dragged
out into the field and burned, and a lot of people went
over and helped, and everybody slept with his windows
closed until the wind shifted. News that Orville had dis-
posed of the owl cheered everybody up, and for the first
time in years people realized that once again they would
have to begin burying hens. But it was worth it. And then
the train came in from Boston one morning, and the big
door opened on the express car, and there was Orville's
owl, crate and all, as big as life and twice as natural. Les
Rogers, the expressman, brought him up and set him on
the lawn, and when Orville went for his mail he had a
letter from Franklin Park, and they thanked him a great
deal, but said they already had an owl. Everybody in town

could see anybody who had an owl wouldn't want two, so Orville built another cage and put the owl in it, and that afternoon nearly everybody in town came around to see the owl again, and most of them brought a hen or a rat or something.

The story runs out about then. The owl got away one night. Some thought Orville did it as a graceful way out. Some thought Mrs. Stevens did it. Somebody did it, because the pen had a good hasp on it, and was padlocked. Nobody ever saw the owl again, and nobody around there ever saw as big an owl again.

The ducks turned out all right. Orville had big flocks of wild mallards right up to the time live decoys were outlawed, and after that he kept a few for old time's sake. Just about every family in town, at one time or another, had some of the mallards either for pets or tollers or both. And so the story of the owl ran its course and came to an end. I said in the beginning that I didn't know how I could show it helped bring me up, but I think it did. One way or another.

He that ruleth his spirit is better than he that taketh a city. *PROVERBS*

Aᴛ LAST, after many things, came that June evening when the Congregational Church was hung with evergreen balsam, and great baskets of field daisies stood roundabout, and the organist struck the first chord of the processional and my class in high school lock-stepped for the baccalaureate address. It was the end of our growing up. The community had done what it could, officially and otherwise, and now we were to have things summed up in a half-hour of admonishing precepts by the new minister.

We had rehearsed for it all week. Stillman Jenkins still couldn't get it down pat, and he humped down the aisle beside Grace Munroe until poor Grace, in confused desperation, humped along with him and couldn't get back into step. But the rest of us had it good. In those days we didn't dignify high school scholarship with the masquerade of cap and gown. The boys had neat blue double-breasted suits—some of them the first suits, and some of them the first long pants. The girls had white dresses, most of them made at home, and some of them hemmed by old Aaron Yeakson who wasn't going to be around to hem many more. The girls had bouquets of lilacs and peonies, and some of them boughten flowers. The marshal's baton flung blue and gold ribbons in time to the organ's triumph, and we got to our seats with more success than anybody had expected.

This new minister was really a good one, and he didn't stay in our town long. He came there to begin his work, and before long he was called to a large and prosperous parish in a distant and populous city, and he has gone on to great things in his ministry. Probably he has forgotten what he said. I know my class hasn't, because not long ago we had one of our reunions, and we talked about it then. His text was, "Write the vision, and make it plain upon the tables, that he may run that readeth it."

He told about the wonderful growing up we had—here in this quiet coastal town where so many fine qualities and virtues had come together in the people, and things were plain upon the tables if we could recognize the values and build them into our lives. He told us that great deeds among many men are not always the greatest success—but that we would do well to live by contentment and happiness, and take pleasure in the way of life that had produced us. He talked about the ocean and the forest, the flights of birds and the wild berries, the rising moon and the coming of storms, and the green of growing things after the snows and cold. He spoke of the people whose vision had been written plain before us—and he called many of them by name. Some of them were in the church, all of them were familiar friends. He told about the work we did as a town, and how we lived together. He talked of playtime—the picnics and sociables. He told us the time was coming when the world would know little of the things we knew. He bade us go forth, and never forget that our childhood had been such that men would envy us. As for school, he said, we could go on to higher things, but those of us who didn't would always have our little town in our lives, and wherever we were, at any time, we would know more and more as time went on, that our town had made us—and made us well. "Write the vision," he said, "and write it plain, because people will read what you write, and they will know it was an uncommon growing-up that wrote it."

Then there was another prayer, and the organist struck a chord again, and we marched out of the church and on into whatever the world had for us. Some of us stayed in the little town, and some will stay there always. All of us remember these things, and we know that the minister was right. Willy-nilly, wherever we are, the vision is set down plain, because nothing will ever take that little town out of our lives.

After I got home that night Mother said, "Hang that suit up, and take the things out of the pockets."

Father said it was a good sermon, he hadn't ever thought of it that way. Mother said, "We won't keep that minister in this town very long."

Father said, "No, but he's never going to forget he was here."

And I happen to know he hasn't.

But Mother came into my room after I was in bed and sat and talked to me, and she said, "That was a nice time tonight, and you all did very well."

When she leaned over in the dark to kiss me good night, a warm tear fell on my forehead.

9172207